CoDA Blue Book Pocket Edition
Co-Dependents Anonymous, Abridged

For general information about CoDA,
please write or call:
Co-Dependents Anonymous, Inc.
P.O. Box 33577
Phoenix, AZ 85067-3577
USA
Phone: 602-277-7991
Toll Free: 888-444-2359
www.coda.org

This is CoDA Conference endorsed literature
Copyright© 2016
All Rights Reserved.
This publication may not be reproduced
or photocopied without written permission
of Co-Dependents Anonymous, Inc.

For additional copies of this book, or to order other CoDA
Conference endorsed literature, contact:
CoRe Publications
P.O. Box 1004
Denver, NC 28037-1004
USA
Phone: 704-483-3038
Fax: 704-483-3088
E-mail: coreorders@gmail.com
Online ordering: www.coda.org/index.cfm/purchase/
Kindle E-book available at amazon.com

To a loving Higher Power

*To each member of the Fellowship
of Co-Dependents Anonymous*

To the codependent who still suffers

Acknowledgments

We, the members of the Fellowship of Co-Dependents Anonymous, would like to express our heartfelt appreciation and gratitude to all who have committed time, energy, gifts, and talents to CoDA. To you who worked so diligently to develop and establish CoDA as a program of recovery from codependence, and to you who continue to arduously support and maintain CoDA's growth, we say "Thank you."

The heritage of the Twelve Steps and Twelve Traditions of CoDA are found in the program of Alcoholics Anonymous. We wish to express our sincere gratitude to Bill W. and Dr. Bob, the founders of A.A., and to the successors of Alcoholics Anonymous for the work you have accomplished, the struggles you have endured, and the successes you have experienced as you walked this path before us.

The Twelve Steps and Twelve Traditions are reprinted and adapted with permission of Alcoholics Anonymous World Services, Inc. Permission to reprint and adapt this material does not mean that A.A. has reviewed or approved the content of this publication, nor that A.A. agrees with the views expressed herein. A.A. is a program of recovery from alcoholism *only*—use of the Twelve Steps and Twelve Traditions in connection with programs and activities which are patterned after A.A., but which address other problems, does not imply otherwise.

CONTENTS

Foreword i
Preamble ii
Welcome iii
Twelve Steps of Co-Dependents Anonymous iv
Twelve Traditions of Co-Dependents Anonymous v
Twelve Steps of Alcoholics Anonymous vi
Twelve Traditions of Alcoholics Anonymous vi
Twelve Promises of Co-Dependents Anonymous vii

Chapter 1
    Beginning Our Journey 1

Chapter 2
    Our Spiritual Dilemma 15

Chapter 3
    A Suggested Program of Recovery 25

Chapter 4
    Service to Others 85

Chapter 5
    Commonly Asked Questions 97

APPENDICES
1. CoDA'S First Six Years 129
2. How to Get in Touch With CoDA 141
3. CoDA Materials Available from CoRe 142

Foreword

Co-Dependents Anonymous is a worldwide Fellowship of men and women who come together to solve their common and individual problems of codependence. The need for such a program as CoDA was so great that in the first six years of CoDA's existence the program grew to more than 4,000 meetings worldwide, with a membership of approximately 100,000.

In the infancy of Co-Dependents Anonymous, the Board of Trustees turned to the founders to draft the first version of a book to reflect the experience, strength, and hope of the Fellowship. This version began the process leading to the book you're reading today. This book, *Co-Dependents Anonymous,* is the culmination of many years of work involving members of several Boards of Trustees and others in the Fellowship. This work is not a product of any one time or place. It is an ongoing evolutionary process, produced by countless meetings of group conscience.

We offer this book, not only as a practical guide, but as a symbol of our own collective journey. It represents a cross section of our experiences, both joyous and painful, and it stands as a beacon to the codependent who still suffers. There is hope for changed relationships with a Higher Power, ourselves, and others. We can move out of our current, perhaps lifelong pain and into a new way of living.

We now invite all who suffer from codependence to read our book in the hope that each of you may find what many of us have found—the hope and freedom of recovery.

Preamble

Co-Dependents Anonymous is a Fellowship of men and women whose common purpose is to develop healthy relationships. The only requirement for membership is a desire for healthy and loving relationships. We gather together to support and share with each other in a journey of self-discovery—learning to love the self. Living the program allows each of us to become increasingly honest with ourselves about our personal histories and our own codependent behaviors.

We rely upon the Twelve Steps and Twelve Traditions for knowledge and wisdom. These are the principles of our program and guides to developing honest and fulfilling relationships with ourselves and others. In CoDA, we each learn to build a bridge to a Higher Power of our own understanding, and we allow others the same privilege.

This renewal process is a gift of healing for us. By actively working the program of Co-Dependents Anonymous, we can each realize a new joy, acceptance, and serenity in our lives.

Welcome

We welcome you to Co-Dependents Anonymous, a program of recovery from codependence, where each of us may share our experience, strength, and hope in our efforts to find freedom where there has been bondage, and peace where there has been turmoil, in our relationships with others and ourselves.

Most of us have been searching for ways to overcome the dilemmas of the conflicts in our relationships and our childhoods. Many of us were raised in families where addictions existed—some of us were not. In either case, we have found in each of our lives that codependence is a most deeply-rooted, compulsive behavior, and that it is born out of our sometimes moderately, sometimes extremely dysfunctional family systems.

We have each experienced in our own ways the painful trauma of the emptiness of our childhood and relationships throughout our lives. We attempted to use others—our mates, our friends, and even our children, as our sole source of identity, value, and well-being, and as a way of trying to restore within us the emotional losses from our childhoods. Our histories may include other powerful addictions, which at times we have used to cope with our codependence.

We have all learned to survive life, but in CoDA we are learning to live life. Through applying the Twelve Steps and principles found in CoDA to our daily lives and relationships—both present and past—we can experience a new freedom from our self-defeating lifestyles. It is an individual growth process. Each of us is growing at our own pace and will continue to do so as we remain open to God's will for us on a daily basis. Our sharing is our way of identification and helps us to free the emotional bonds of our past and the compulsive control of our present.

No matter how traumatic your past or despairing your present may seem, there is hope for a new day in the program of Co-Dependents Anonymous. No longer do you need to rely on others as a power greater than yourself. May you instead find here a new strength within to be that which God intended—precious and free.

The Twelve Steps of Co-Dependents Anonymous*

1. We admitted we were powerless over others—that our lives had become unmanageable.
2. Came to believe that a power greater than ourselves could restore us to sanity.
3. Made a decision to turn our will and our lives over to the care of God as we understood God.
4. Made a searching and fearless moral inventory of ourselves.
5. Admitted to God, to ourselves, and to another human being the exact nature of our wrongs.
6. Were entirely ready to have God remove all these defects of character.
7. Humbly asked God to remove our shortcomings.
8. Made a list of all persons we had harmed, and became willing to make amends to them all.
9. Made direct amends to such people wherever possible, except when to do so would injure them or others.
10. Continued to take personal inventory and when we were wrong promptly admitted it.
11. Sought through prayer and meditation to improve our conscious contact with God as we understood God, praying only for knowledge of God's will for us and the power to carry that out.
12. Having had a spiritual awakening as the result of these steps, we tried to carry this message to other codependents, and to practice these principles in all our affairs.

*The Twelve Steps and Twelve Traditions are reprinted and adapted with permission of Alcoholics Anonymous World Services, Inc. Permission to reprint and adapt this material does not mean that A.A. has reviewed or approved the content of this publication, nor that A.A. agrees with the views expressed herein. A.A. is a program of recovery from alcoholism *only*—use of the Twelve Steps and Twelve Traditions in connection with programs and activities which are patterned after A.A., but which address other problems, does not imply otherwise.

The Twelve Traditions of Co-Dependents Anonymous*

1. Our common welfare should come first; personal recovery depends upon CoDA unity.
2. For our group purpose there is but one ultimate authority—a loving Higher Power as expressed to our group conscience. Our leaders are but trusted servants; they do not govern.
3. The only requirement for membership in CoDA is a desire for healthy and loving relationships.
4. Each group should remain autonomous except in matters affecting other groups or CoDA as a whole.
5. Each group has but one primary purpose—to carry its message to other codependents who still suffer.
6. A CoDA group ought never endorse, finance or lend the CoDA name to any related facility or outside enterprise, lest problems of money, property and prestige divert us from our primary spiritual aim.
7. Every CoDA group ought to be fully self-supporting, declining outside contributions.
8. Co-Dependents Anonymous should remain forever nonprofessional, but our service centers may employ special workers.
9. CoDA, as such, ought never be organized; but we may create service boards or committees directly responsible to those they serve.
10. CoDA has no opinion on outside issues; hence the CoDA name ought never be drawn into public controversy.
11. Our public relations policy is based on attraction rather than promotion; we need always maintain personal anonymity at the level of press, radio and films.
12. Anonymity is the spiritual foundation of all our Traditions, ever reminding us to place principles before personalities.

*The Twelve Steps and Twelve Traditions are reprinted and adapted with permission of Alcoholics Anonymous World Services, Inc. Permission to reprint and adapt this material does not mean that A.A. has reviewed or approved the content of this publication, nor that A.A. agrees with the views expressed herein. A.A. is a program of recovery from alcoholism *only*—use of the Twelve Steps and Twelve Traditions in connection with programs and activities which are patterned after A.A., but which address other problems, does not imply otherwise.

The Twelve Steps of Alcoholics Anonymous

1. We admitted we were powerless over alcohol, that our lives had become unmanageable. 2. Came to believe that a Power greater than ourselves could restore us to sanity. 3. Made a decision to turn our will and our lives over to the care of God *as we understood Him*. 4. Made a searching and fearless moral inventory of ourselves. 5. Admitted to God, to ourselves, and to another human being the exact nature of our wrongs. 6. Were entirely ready to have God remove all these defects of character. 7. Humbly asked Him to remove our shortcomings. 8. Made a list of all persons we had harmed, and became willing to make amends to them all. 9. Made direct amends to such people wherever possible, except when to do so would injure them or others. 10. Continued to take personal inventory and when we were wrong promptly admitted it. 11. Sought through prayer and meditation to improve our conscious contact with God *as we understood Him*, praying only for knowledge of His will for us and the power to carry that out. 12. Having had a spiritual awakening as the result of these steps, we tried to carry this message to alcoholics, and to practice these principles in all our affairs.

The Twelve Traditions of Alcoholics Anonymous

1. Our common welfare should come first; personal recovery depends upon A.A. unity. 2. For our group purpose there is but one ultimate authority—a loving God as He may express Himself in our group conscience. Our leaders are but trusted servants; they do not govern. 3. The only requirement for A.A. membership is a desire to stop drinking. 4. Each group should be autonomous except in matters affecting other groups or A.A. as a whole. 5. Each group has but one primary purpose—to carry its message to the alcoholic who still suffers. 6. An A.A. group ought never endorse, finance or lend the A.A. name to any related facility or outside enterprise, lest problems of money, property and prestige divert us from our primary purpose. 7. Every A.A. group ought to be fully self-supporting, declining outside contributions. 8. Alcoholics Anonymous should remain forever nonprofessional, but our service centers may employ special workers. 9. A.A. as such, ought never be organized; but we may create service boards or committees directly responsible to those they serve. 10. Alcoholics Anonymous has no opinion on outside issues; hence the A.A. name ought never be drawn into public controversy. 11. Our public relations policy is based on attraction rather than promotion; we need always maintain personal anonymity at the level of press, radio and films. 12. Anonymity is the spiritual foundation of all our Traditions, ever reminding us to place principles before personalities.

The Twelve Promises of Co-Dependents Anonymous

I can expect a miraculous change in my life by working the program of Co-Dependents Anonymous. As I make an honest effort to work the Twelve Steps and follow the Twelve Traditions...

1. I know a new sense of belonging. The feelings of emptiness and loneliness will disappear.
2. I am no longer controlled by my fears. I overcome my fears and act with courage, integrity and dignity.
3. I know a new freedom.
4. I release myself from worry, guilt and regret about my past and present. I am aware enough not to repeat it.
5. I know a new love and acceptance of myself and others. I feel genuinely lovable, loving and loved.
6. I learn to see myself as equal to others. My new and renewed relationships are all with equal partners.
7. I am capable of developing and maintaining healthy and loving relationships. The need to control and manipulate others will disappear as I learn to trust those who are trustworthy.
8. I learn that it is possible for me to mend—to become more loving, intimate and supportive. I have the choice of communicating with my family in a way which is safe for me and respectful of them.
9. I acknowledge that I am a unique and precious creation.
10. I no longer need to rely solely on others to provide my sense of worth.
11. I trust the guidance I receive from my Higher Power and come to believe in my own capabilities.
12. I gradually experience serenity, strength, and spiritual growth in my daily life.

CHAPTER ONE

Beginning Our Journey

Perhaps some of these thoughts are yours...

"If he/she changed, everything would be all right."

"I can't control this pain, these people and what's happening."

"It's all my fault."

"I keep getting into the same bad relationships."

"I feel so empty and lost."

"Who am I?"

"What's wrong with me?"

Our sadness and loss bring us here. We want change, and we want it now. We want to escape our misery. We want to feel good about ourselves and live abundant, fulfilling lives. We want happy, healthy relationships.

If any of the preceding thoughts are yours, then you're not alone. Many of us in the Fellowship of Co-Dependents Anonymous have felt deep sadness, anxiety, despair, and depression and have turned here—to each other and a Higher Power—for our sanity to be restored.

What brings us here may be a crisis such as divorce, separation, imprisonment, health problems or attempt at suicide. Some of us are feeling weary, desperate or devastated.

If you're new to recovery, this moment may not seem like something to remember, but someday you might consider it a celebration. Many of us find our pain to be a gift, for without these feelings of emptiness and despair, we can't experience a real desire to change our lives. Without this desire, many of us know we won't make the decision to change. We want balance, happiness and peace, but to change we must acknowledge these feelings and decide to climb out of this pit of pain.

Once we make this decision, many of us ask, "How do I go about this change? Where can I get help?" At first, many of us think we can solve our problems by just trying harder or by studying techniques to change people. Often our pride or upbringing cause us to think that we can do this ourselves. These two approaches, however, block our road to a better way of life.

What is codependence?

Somewhere along this road we learn about codependence. We hear about it from a friend or therapist. We see it mentioned in the news. Many of us wonder if codependence describes who we are.

Codependence is a disease that deteriorates our souls. It affects our personal lives, our families, children, friends, relatives, our businesses and careers, our health, and our spiritual growth. It is debilitating and, if left untreated, causes us to become more destructive to ourselves and others. Many of us come to a point when we must look beyond ourselves for help.

When we attend our first meeting of Co-Dependents Anonymous, many of us find a source for help. Each of us arrives here from different directions. Some of us are urged by family members or friends. Some of us come to CoDA when our physicians, psychiatrists, or therapists see the need. Many of us reach CoDA's doorstep after treatment for codependence or other addictions.

Whether it's crisis or curiosity that brings us to CoDA, many of us learn about the characteristics of codependence at our first meeting. These characteristics help us determine what unhealthy patterns weave in and out of our lives. Do we live in extremes instead of balance? How do we, our mates, children and friends suffer because of our behaviors? Do our codependent behaviors cause our relationships to stagnate, deteriorate or destruct? If the answers to these soul-searching questions cause us to admit, "I am codependent and I need help," then we're beginning to locate recovery's path.

It all begins with an honest look at ourselves.

The following characteristics of codependence outlined in the CoDA pamphlet, "What is CoDA?" can help us to identify to what degree this illness affects us:

> Many of us struggle with the questions: What is codependence? Am I codependent? We want precise definitions and diagnostic criteria before we will decide. As stated in the Eighth Tradition, Co-Dependents Anonymous

is a nonprofessional Fellowship. We offer no definition or diagnostic criteria for codependence. What we do offer from our experience are characteristic attitudes and behaviors that describe what our codependent histories have been like. We believe that recovery begins with an honest self-diagnosis. We come to accept our inability to maintain healthy and nurturing relationships with ourselves and others. We begin to recognize that the cause lies in long-standing destructive patterns of living.

These patterns and characteristics are offered as a tool to aid in self-evaluation. They may be particularly helpful to newcomers.

Denial Patterns: Codependents often...

- have difficulty identifying what they are feeling.
- minimize, alter, or deny how they truly feel.
- perceive themselves as completely unselfish and dedicated to the well-being of others.
- lack empathy for the feelings and needs of others.
- label others with their negative traits.
- think they can take care of themselves without any help from others.
- mask pain in various ways such as anger, humor, or isolation.
- express negativity or aggression in indirect and passive ways.

- do not recognize the unavailability of those people to whom they are attracted.

Low Self-esteem Patterns: Codependents often...

- have difficulty making decisions.
- judge what they think, say, or do harshly, as never good enough.
- are embarrassed to receive recognition, praise, or gifts.
- value others' approval of their thinking, feelings, and behavior over their own.
- do not perceive themselves as lovable or worthwhile persons.
- seek recognition and praise to overcome feeling less than.
- have difficulty admitting a mistake.
- need to appear to be right in the eyes of others and may even lie to look good.
- are unable to identify or ask for what they need and want.
- perceive themselves as superior to others.
- look to others to provide their sense of safety.
- have difficulty getting started, meeting deadlines, and completing projects.
- have trouble setting healthy priorities and boundaries.

Compliance Patterns: Codependents often...
- are extremely loyal, remaining in harmful situations too long.
- compromise their own values and integrity to avoid rejection or anger.
- put aside their own interests in order to do what others want.
- are hypervigilant regarding the feelings of others and take on those feelings.
- are afraid to express their beliefs, opinions, and feelings when they differ from those of others.
- accept sexual attention when they want love.
- make decisions without regard to the consequences.
- give up their truth to gain the approval of others or to avoid change.

Control Patterns: Codependents often...
- believe people are incapable of taking care of themselves.
- attempt to convince others what to think, do, or feel.
- freely offer advice and direction without being asked.
- become resentful when others decline their help or reject their advice.
- lavish gifts and favors on those they want to influence.
- use sexual attention to gain approval and acceptance.

- have to feel needed in order to have a relationship with others.
- demand that their needs be met by others.
- use charm and charisma to convince others of their capacity to be caring and compassionate.
- use blame and shame to exploit others emotionally.
- refuse to cooperate, compromise, or negotiate.
- adopt an attitude of indifference, helplessness, authority, or rage to manipulate outcomes.
- use recovery jargon in an attempt to control the behavior of others.
- pretend to agree with others to get what they want.

Avoidance Patterns: Codependents often...

- act in ways that invite others to reject, shame, or express anger toward them.
- judge harshly what others think, say, or do.
- avoid emotional, physical, or sexual intimacy as a way to maintain distance.
- allow addictions to people, places, and things to distract them from achieving intimacy in relationships.
- use indirect or evasive communication to avoid conflict or confrontation.

- diminish their capacity to have healthy relationships by declining to use the tools of recovery.

- suppress their feelings or needs to avoid feeling vulnerable.

- pull people toward them, but when others get close, push them away.

- refuse to give up their self-will to avoid surrendering to a power greater than themselves.

- believe displays of emotion are a sign of weakness.

- withhold expressions of appreciation.

Many of us are shocked when we read this list because many of the characteristics describe us. Some of us are relieved to see these feelings and behaviors on paper because there's hope we might have discovered a way out of our pain. Some of us are embarrassed, as though someone is reading our personal mail or journals. We wonder, "How did they find out?" and, "If these are the characteristics of codependence, then the whole world is codependent."

At our first meeting, we listen to people talk about their struggles and how their lives have changed from working a program of recovery. We hear of relationships healing—those with ourselves, our Higher Power, and others. We learn how we can experience freedom and an inner peace.

We listen with wonder as they seem to be telling our stories, describing our problems, and talking about our most secret feelings. This may be one of the few times we don't feel strange or alone. Armed with the knowledge that we're like other people, we realize that if they can work the program and improve their lives, we can too. As we attend more meetings, we hear a message of hope loud and clear; we hear it through CoDA literature and the stories of those around us. This message of hope tells us that we can also have the gifts of recovery, if we're willing.

We also learn that all of us suffer from this illness to some degree, so recognizing codependence can be difficult. Understanding codependent behaviors and attitudes can be especially tough because many of them are not destructive; as children we may have used these behaviors to survive abuse or neglect. For example, we might have developed internal detectors to read our parents' moods and then developed behaviors based on their moods to keep them happy.

For many of us, codependence became worse as we grew up. Behaviors that may have served us well in childhood are now causing our lives to deteriorate. As our codependence gets worse, we lose our ability to acknowledge this pain and its harm.

Once we acknowledge our feelings of pain, we can begin to make the decision to change. We must also try to be patient, loving, and forgiving of ourselves while we begin this road to recovery. Each of us will recover in unique ways and at a different pace. Our paths are as individual as our personalities and circumstances, but while we start from different points, we share a common recovery goal.

The Fellowship of CoDA

The road to recovery is filled with fellowship; the people of Co-Dependents Anonymous become our dear companions on our journey. Where we may have felt isolated and helpless, we can now feel friendship and strength.

One of the program's greatest blessings is this journey we take together. We try to understand and support one another. We're able to renew our trust and faith in humanity; we see growth in people who work the program and look to the Fellowship of CoDA for support.

New faces are always welcome at CoDA. They give us hope because we know more people will journey with us to live more fulfilling lives. In CoDA, there is understanding and acceptance, not judgment and advice.

With the love, support, and safety the CoDA Fellowship provides, we can begin to describe our own codependent characteristics and discover their sources. We learn to accept the support and guidance from others and begin to trust in a Higher Power or God of our own definition. We acknowledge our troubled past and accept where it might have begun. For many of us, this can be found in the abuse and neglect we experienced in our significant childhood relationships. We may be reluctant to call some of these experiences "abuse" and "neglect," but we might need to recognize them as part of our personal history.

These issues might apply not only to our childhood—emotionally and physically—but sexually, intellectually, and spiritually as well. They affect us as adults in our ability to love ourselves and others, and to be loved. We often get caught in negative situations that impact our mental and physical health and the well-being of others. Some of us may be unable to recognize our feelings and comprehend the disastrous path we're on. We call this denial.

Denial

Denial of ourselves—our past and present—is often a great stumbling block to our early recovery. It's a term often used when we don't accept our codependent behaviors as we learn about their patterns and characteristics or as we hear them described in another person's story. Often in our frustration, we clearly see what everyone else is doing wrong, but we can't recognize our own wrongdoing. Some of us come to a place of despair and think of nothing else but giving up. We isolate from our friends and families, many times rejecting their love. Some of us go to elaborate degrees to create the "all together" act in our homes, marriages, families, jobs, friendships, and social lives. Try as we might to do otherwise, we often experience devastating marriages, parenting and family relationships, friendships, and careers. Sometimes, even then, our denial continues.

We may become so entangled in denial and control that we're forced to accept the hand of recovery through formal intervention and treatment. Eventually, we may get involved in separation or divorce, legal action, imprisonment, attempted suicide, hospitalization for physically related illnesses, mental problems, job loss or a sidelined career. We walk an extremely lonely and empty path in denial, whether we suffer severe devastation or try to appear "all together."

We usually reach a point where denial no longer works. We finally determine "enough is enough." We seek the hand of others in CoDA and, if necessary, professional help.

Acceptance

As we break through our denial, we're better able to determine the degree of our problem. We recognize our denial as a symptom of codependence and see it as a process that continually emerges, subsides and evolves throughout our lives.

As we continue our recovery in CoDA, we replace denial with acceptance. We progressively embrace our past and current life with honesty, openness, and a willingness to change. We move beyond denial and identify the harm our codependent decisions and behaviors have caused us personally, as well as our families, careers, physical health, and spirituality. We see how codependence has allowed us to become trapped in unhealthy situations and relationships. It affects every aspect of our lives. As we see our direction more clearly, we recognize that our journey is not advanced by force, will, intellect or even strength of character. At some point, most of us acknowledge a Higher Power as the guide on our journey, the source of our progress. We may become more aware that we're on a spiritual journey.

We know we're not alone when we accept our codependence. Together, we're learning how to love and be loved, and how to live life rather than merely survive it. Recovery in CoDA is an ongoing process. It's a life that constantly challenges us. Recovery isn't earned like a merit badge; it's a way of living that evolves with us every day.

The *Serenity Prayer* expresses our awareness that recovery is about living life as it unfolds. These simple phrases affirm that our recovery is lived one moment, one decision, one day at a time:

> *God, grant me the Serenity to*
> *accept the things I cannot change;*
> *Courage to change the things I can;*
> *and Wisdom to know the difference.*

Some of us become nervous at the mention of spirituality and a Higher Power. Even if you've given up on a Higher Power or wonder if such a being exists, you are welcome to the program of Co-Dependents Anonymous. This is not a religious program, but a spiritual one; it's a program for finding peace within. Over time, most everyone who makes a conscious choice to work this spiritual program decides what their Higher Power should be.

With the help of a loving Higher Power, the program of Co-Dependents Anonymous, and those who join us on this journey, each of us can experience the hope of recovery. We find the willingness to change, grow, and evolve toward the positive, loving potential that lies within us. Through the guidance of our Higher Power, the program of Co-Dependents Anonymous, and the CoDA family, each of us can experience the hope of recovery and a life filled with peace and joy.

CHAPTER 2

Our Spiritual Dilemma

Codependence causes a dilemma to boil inside us. For many of us, our pain and despair are signs of a deep inner need. This need, hunger or desire gnaws at the core of our being. It could be a cry for unconditional love, respect, nurturing, acceptance, or joy. Many of us turn to other people, drugs, alcohol, or other addictions to fill this need to gain some sense of safety, self-worth, and well-being.

Our answers to the following questions can help us determine how we've looked to other people or addictions for our emotional well-being.

- Do I control others to relieve my fears?
- Do I let others control me for fear of their abuse or neglect?
- Do I adapt or change my behavior for others?
- Do I validate my value and worth as a person through them?
- Do I avoid others in order to feel safe?

In CoDA, we learn that our self-worth and well-being come from our Higher Power. When we attempt to codependently control or manipulate others, we turn ourselves into a Higher Power to maintain our sense of safety and well-being. When we codependently avoid others, as well as adapt or change our behavior for others, we give them, instead of our Higher Power, this control and strength.

As we turn ourselves into a Higher Power or give this power to others, we leave little room for our Higher Power to work in our lives. This is our spiritual dilemma.

The following paragraphs describe how our spiritual dilemma may involve control and avoidance, especially when circumstances become stressful.

Controlling people and circumstances
Many of us take pride in controlling circumstances and those around us. If we think we might be abandoned, abused, or neglected by others, we label them as the problem and manipulate them. Specifically, we may over control our mates, children, family members, friends, or associates by dominating them. Another way we control them is by being "nice," passive or quiet for long periods of time. Then, when fear or other feelings overwhelm us, we rage, isolate, or allow others to act out our feelings for us.

We become a Higher Power when we control others, to any degree, either quietly or aggressively. We may even reinforce our control with an attitude of arrogance, authority, or prejudice. We value others' beliefs and behaviors as foolish, selfish, or worthless. We establish ourselves in a "better-than" position. Our way is the only way, we think.

In giving the power of our Higher Power to other people, we may seek others' approval, often to the point of abandoning our own needs and desires. We live in fear of those we put in power. We dread their anger or disapproving looks. We fear their disappointment, avoidance, or control. In essence, we lose our sense of self (or never gain it) because we become obsessed with their attitudes and behaviors toward us.

Avoiding people and circumstances

Some of us may fear others so much that we avoid any degree of closeness or intimacy. We work hard to prevent placing ourselves in a vulnerable position. We become skilled at hiding our fears, especially when things seem out of control. We may remain silent even when we experience injustice or abuse.

We may fall into martyr roles or act helpless to avoid confrontation or accountability. We may place ourselves in a subservient position and judge ourselves harshly. We may believe we're not acceptable enough to live a life with relationships, purpose or happiness.

Our codependence worsens; our fear and shame overwhelm us. We control and avoid others even more. But these behaviors are temporary fixes; our fears always return and our shame is ever present.

Many of us seek false gods. We numb our feelings with alcohol, drugs, food, sex, or work; these often turn into chronic addictions and compound our problems. None of them provide us freedom or peace.

Regardless of whether we position ourselves as "better than" or "less than," as a controller or avoider, we behave in self-centered ways. Equality is lost.

What drives our need to control and avoid others?

Many of us ask, "Aren't some of these behaviors healthy?" The answer can be found in the motivation for our behaviors. Our behaviors toward ourselves, others and our Higher Power may be appropriate if they are by choice with healthy boundaries. For example, we may leave the premises of a person who is verbally or physically threatening us. We behave codependently, however, if we allow fear or shame to dictate our lives, causing us to rely on past survival instincts such as control and avoidance.

Fear

For many of us, fear is our guardian; it helps protect us from harm. As codependents, we habitually use fear to protect ourselves from any opportunity of being shamed by others. Our fear may be cloaked in anger or resentment, rage, pain, or loneliness. Oftentimes our passivity, silence, manipulation, isolation, rage, violence, denial, or even deceit, are our expressions of fear. Other feelings that show up as fear are: concern, anxiety, nervousness, and feeling uptight or scared.

Shame

Shame causes us to believe we are "less than," stupid, foolish, worthless, inadequate, or unwanted. It diminishes our true sense of identity and destroys our belief that we are loving human beings. It erodes our self-esteem and sense of equality in the world.

Experiencing fear and shame as children

As children, our identity as well as our relationships with our Higher Power, ourselves, and others were damaged each time we were abused or neglected. We felt shame and naturally feared its reoccurrence, yet we allowed our sense of self and well-being to be shaped by those who abused and neglected us. As children, we had no choice.

As we continued to experience abuse or neglect, our fear and shame intensified; we gave more of ourselves away. Over time (most often without our knowing), our abusers became our Higher Power. We learned to fear their authority. As the abuse and neglect continued, the possibility of developing an emotionally fulfilling relationship with ourselves, others, and our Higher Power diminished.

We learned survival skills in order to cope. We controlled or avoided potentially volatile circumstances. We cast away our childhood, tried to become little adults, or rebelled. Many of us didn't understand our actions because they were often instinctive.

Over time, we learned how to alleviate our fear and shame by controlling and/or avoiding ourselves and others. When we felt overwhelmed or stressed out, we relied on what we knew best to survive. In this devastating codependent cycle, we took greater control of life, allowing less room for a power greater than ourselves to work through us.

Continuing this behavior as adults

Without some form of help, we carry these emotional conflicts and survival patterns into our adult lives. We hope to find peace and happiness and leave the past behind; but instead, we recreate similar or opposite circumstances in our adult relationships. Neither extreme is healthy. We unknowingly transfer the characteristics and power of our childhood abusers to significant people in our lives today. Sometimes we transfer abusive characteristics to our Higher Power, too.

In our adult relationships, we fearfully guard against any sign of shame, abuse, or neglect. We become manipulative or avoid other people and circumstances. This fear can grow stronger than the shame itself. It forms a shaky foundation for relationships. We continue to draw others near us (hoping for intimacy) but when they get too close, we push them away because of our fear of shame.

Building our own concept of a Higher Power

Many of us participate in organized religions or learn various doctrines and concepts of God or a Higher Power. Some of us may hope to cleanse our sense of shame by living righteous lives. Even controlled behavioral change combined with our religious beliefs are not enough. Our motives may be virtuous, but we're still emotionally bound to the abusive, neglectful people in our lives—most deeply to those from our childhood.

Some of us are atheists or agnostics. Organized religion may remind us of an abusive, authoritarian God. Some of us may be angry at our Higher Power for the negative experiences we faced, or we may discover we've been angry at this Higher Power for years but didn't know it. Some of us believe we're undeserving of God's love or grace.

We must ask ourselves, "Is my life filled with honesty and serenity?" "Am I working toward a safe, healthy, and loving relationship with my Higher Power, myself and others?" Most often, we say, "No." Our fear and shame drive us to behave in devastating ways.

Wherever our codependent course takes us, we find we're left with no other recourse than to seek a safe power greater than ourselves—one that can restore us to sanity. To continue recovery, we must become willing to consider this endeavor.

If we haven't experienced a Higher Power before, our concept of a safe being can begin to take shape. If we already have a relationship with God, we can help strengthen it. Whatever our past beliefs, we can begin building a spiritual foundation for our program of recovery.

Beginning the journey of recovery from codependence

In our codependence, we excessively place our faith and hope in ourselves, our mates, children, relatives, and friends—even our careers and lifestyles. We do this for our safety, value, worth, and well-being.

In recovery, we learn to build faith and hope, and progressively surrender our lives to the care of a loving Higher Power. We learn to let go of our controlling and avoidance behaviors, to resolve our feelings about what we do, and to emotionally detach from those on whom we compulsively rely.

Some of us gladly reach for our Higher Power's hand. Some of us reach in desperation. Some of us realize that our ability to trust anyone or anything has been so greatly diminished that it may take time. We may need to feel some sense of safety. We may have to act as if we have faith until it becomes a reality.

Many of us pray or meditate when our fear is so overwhelming that we're unable to surrender even a small part of our will or lives to our Higher Power. Often, time will allow only a simple prayer such as, "God, please help me find the willingness to let go."

As we continue our recovery, many of us can surrender more easily to our Higher Power and experience this power's heartfelt presence within us. Surrendering and letting go doesn't mean that life's circumstances will happen the way we want. It means we're better able to accept life as it is and handle problems with a newfound strength from our Higher Power. This enables us to experience a growing personal empowerment and a humble, yet truer, self-esteem.

We learn that our Higher Power doesn't create bad people. Goodness dwells within us all, even those responsible for the broken promises and betrayals, abuses, hurts, and fears of our past. It's possible to love these persons, yet not condone their negative behaviors. We can even love and forgive ourselves. In our own way, we're all learning how to love and be loved.

Even with our Higher Power's help, none of us loves or lives life perfectly. Our humanity continues to evolve. We begin to realize that perfectionism is merely an illusion. Over the long haul, we make many mistakes and, at times, "slip" into our former codependent behaviors.

When we're unable to maintain our emotional balance, strength or self-esteem, we reflect on the work we must do and that recovery is a lifelong process. We remember that comparing our progress with others is self-defeating; each of us is learning at our own balance and pace.

To keep our relationship with our Higher Power in perspective, we find it helpful to prioritize our relationships. Our relationship with our Higher Power must come first. Once we establish and begin to develop this relationship, we're better able to develop one with ourselves. As the relationships with our Higher Power and ourselves gain in strength and balance, we begin to heal and develop loving relationships with others. When we accept a healthier priority for our close relationships, we allow our Higher Power to work in our lives. We draw on strengths that far exceed our own.

As we continue to strengthen our relationship with our Higher Power throughout our recovery, our overwhelming tiredness, depression, anxiety, despair, and hopelessness are replaced with an increasing strength and resiliency. Step by step, our fear of shame diminishes. Our childhood wounds and feelings progressively heal. We experience richer encounters of prayer and meditation. It becomes easier to let go of our control and avoidance behaviors, and to allow our Higher Power to guide our life's journey.

The miracles of recovery unfold. Loving relationships with our Higher Power, ourselves and others improve and evolve. We begin to feel more assured that our deepest needs will be cared for. We don't turn as often to other people or to an unhealthy lifestyle to satisfy our spiritual hunger. Like the light of dawn, our Higher Power's will radiates through us with reassurance and trust.

CHAPTER THREE

A Suggested Program of Recovery

Codependence is an illusive and devastating problem that requires simple yet specific solutions. Many of us believe these solutions can be found within the program of Co-Dependents Anonymous. The CoDA program consists of the following: the Fellowship, CoDA meetings, sponsorship, literature, conferences, conventions, service work, the CoDA Twelve Steps and Twelve Traditions.

The CoDA Twelve Steps have been adapted from the Twelve Steps of Alcoholics Anonymous for our use, as well as for many other Twelve Step programs. Millions of people worldwide have applied these concepts to their lives.

These Steps hold the strength and spirit of personal recovery. We become willing to work them to the best of our ability. We're as honest as possible with ourselves, our Higher Power, and another person. Halfhearted attempts to work the Steps often leave us feeling self-defeated; the changes we seek may not last long.

If we attempt to complete the Steps alone, we may perpetuate isolation: a common codependent behavior. In time, many of us seek the loving help of those who have traveled this path before us—sponsors in CoDA who can offer us insight, encouragement, and support. They help us see that these Steps cannot be completed quickly or absolutely; they are not quick fixes.

The Twelve Steps steer us from a path of self-defeating behaviors toward healthy and loving relationships with God, ourselves, and others. They offer us growth, a priority for our relationships, and a guide for living healthy and loving lives. Through their simplistic nature, we can discover who we are and how to become involved in healthy, loving relationships. The Steps help us to see how our past experiences of abuse and neglect have formed and reinforced our codependent behaviors and lifestyles. We learn how to turn over our self-claimed power, addictions, and problems to a loving Higher Power. We give our lives, will, and healing into the care of that Higher Power.

We become accountable for our codependent behaviors which reinforce patterns of devastation in our lives. We grow in humility as we learn of our own shortcomings and defects of character and recognize our skills, talents and successes. From this humble state, we do all within our power to right our wrongs. We also try to complete the work which helps heal our wounds and perhaps those whom we have hurt.

In our Step work, we strive on a daily basis to maintain accountability for our own behavior. We learn to strengthen and deepen our relationship with our Higher Power. We rely more freely upon our Higher Power for our true value, worth, and well-being. Finally, we realize if we want to keep what we've gained through our Step work, we must strive to pass on the experience, strength, and hope of our recovery to those who still suffer from codependence.

Our journey through the Steps may be the most difficult work we ever attempt, yet the rewards and the healing we receive cannot be measured. In time, the Steps become an integral part of our daily lives as we practice these principles in all our affairs.

Listed below are the Twelve Steps which are the suggested program of Co-Dependents Anonymous for personal recovery from codependence:

1. We admitted we were powerless over others—that our lives had become unmanageable.

2. Came to believe that a power greater than ourselves could restore us to sanity.

3. Made a decision to turn our will and our lives over to the care of God as we understood God.

4. Made a searching and fearless moral inventory of ourselves.

5. Admitted to God, to ourselves, and to another human being the exact nature of our wrongs.

6. Were entirely ready to have God remove all these defects of character.

7. Humbly asked God to remove our shortcomings.

8. Made a list of all persons we had harmed, and became willing to make amends to them all.

9. Made direct amends to such people wherever possible, except when to do so would injure them or others.

10. Continued to take personal inventory and, when we were wrong, promptly admitted it.

11. Sought through prayer and meditation to improve our conscious contact with God as we understood God, praying only for knowledge of God's will for us and the power to carry that out.

12. Having had a spiritual awakening as the result of these Steps, we tried to carry this message to other codependents, and to practice these principles in all our affairs.

At first glance, some of us see these Steps as overwhelming tasks that can never be accomplished. Some of us see them as quick, easy instructions that can be achieved in an afternoon or a few days. Some of us avoid them entirely until we become overburdened with crises and our codependent behaviors. Ultimately, we must be willing to move forward and embrace these Steps as part of our personal recovery if we want our lives to get better.

Step One
We admitted we were powerless over others—that our lives had become unmanageable.

On powerlessness—Until now we had applied self-control, obsessiveness, and our own clouded thinking to our problems of living. When our relationships broke down, many of us just tried harder, applying our arsenal of misinformation with a vengeance. Our self-will took many forms. We were overbearing. We were people-pleasers. We conformed. We rebelled. We blamed. We hurt ourselves and we hurt others. Some of us had to go to the edge of insanity or death before we were willing to admit our powerlessness. And all the while we were convinced we were doing the right thing. Where was success?

On unmanageability—Chances are that by the time we reached CoDA our lives were out of control. The coping skills we had relied on for a lifetime were no longer working. We were the victims of a compulsive way of behaving so subtly powerful and damaging that no ordinary means could break it. Our lives were truly unmanageable. It was at this point that our old ideas began to crumble and we became open to the possibility that there might be another way.

excerpt from Step One in the CoDA *Twelve Steps Handbook*

All journeys begin with a first step. Our journey of personal recovery in CoDA begins with the CoDA First Step.

To understand the growing devastation of our powerlessness and unmanageability, we must explore our past and how we arrived at this point. Maybe we're devastated by a divorce, separation, or a loved one's death. Maybe we tried killing ourselves or slowly "bottomed out" from drugs or alcohol. Many of us are overwhelmed and weary. Once we make the decision to change, we start our recovery journey with Step One, the Step of admission and acceptance.

This Step helps us to identify our lifetime of experiences, feelings and behaviors, to pinpoint how we avoid, control and manipulate ourselves, other people and circumstances. We learn how we've become our own Higher Power or placed others in that role. We begin to see that God has not given us the right to control another person's behavior, but we have been given the responsibility to set limits and boundaries for ourselves with others. To explore how we control and avoid ourselves and others, we search our personal histories. We ask ourselves the following questions to see if they apply to our lives:

- What neglect and abuse did I experience growing up?

- Where did I learn to turn my head when I and/or other people were being neglected or abused, and why?

- Who in my childhood displayed these behaviors or instructed me not to tell or share my feelings about it?

- Where did I learn that avoiding others was safer than being involved?

- Where did I learn to control others for my sense of well-being?

- How did I learn that I wasn't good enough or was better than others?

- When, where, and how did I learn to deny my own thoughts, feelings, and needs for the sake of others or, conversely, to demand that the world revolve around me?

- How did I know never to tell the family secrets and why?

- Where did I learn to behave in neglectful and/or abusive ways that are intellectually, emotionally, physically, sexually, and/or spiritually harmful?

- Where did I learn to express these behaviors which are

often communicated in the extremes from silence to violence?

- How did I learn to allow them to be expressed toward me?
- Where and how did I learn that having a relationship would make me whole?
- Did I learn these things through others' words or actions? If so, whose?
- How had I come to survive life through codependent behaviors rather than living life through a sense of freedom?
- What are my true feelings about all of these questions?

By answering these questions, we gain an understanding of how our powerlessness developed in our childhood, but knowing this is not enough. We must see the unmanageability of the codependent behaviors we carry into our adult lives.

To explore our unmanageable adult codependent behaviors, we find it helpful to review the first chapter and its outline of the denial, low self-esteem, control and compliance patterns. We specifically list those patterns which represent our adult codependent behaviors. It's important to be honest with ourselves to change our unmanageability.

By exploring the powerlessness of our childhood and the unmanageability of our adult lives, we come to understand more about our personal heritage. Our denial of codependence fades, our acceptance increases and we're better able to see our destructive adult behaviors.

It is extremely important to remember that our First Step is not to be used to assign blame to others or to ourselves. We're not on a witch-hunt. By holding on to blame, we react codependently and remain powerless.

Rather than blame, we attempt to review our childhood and adult experiences that are the roots of unhealthy behaviors. We acknowledge how powerlessness and unmanageability developed in childhood and gradually manifested themselves in our adult behavior and relationships. We accept that our lives get crazier the more we try to control and avoid ourselves and others. Rather than blame others or ourselves, we become accountable for our feelings about our childhood and adult experiences, as well as our progressive adult codependent behavior.

We find it helpful to list the losses we've experienced in our childhood and adult life. We allow ourselves to grieve these losses—the pain and anger we've held so long. As we release these feelings, we begin to release the energies that drive our codependent behaviors. We see that our codependent behaviors of manipulation, control, and avoidance have only left us in despair.

Many of us share our First Step with our sponsors and friends in recovery. We share our past experiences, losses, and grief. In doing so, we begin to release the emotional depths of our powerlessness and unmanageability. Once we do, we can begin to accept our past, think more positively, and act in healthier ways with ourselves and others.

By understanding and accepting our codependent powerlessness and the unmanageability of our lives, we open the door to possible solutions. We admit that our best efforts in these areas have failed and that we need greater help than our own limited abilities can provide.

From this position of admission and acceptance, we are ready to reach for the help of a power greater than ourselves to restore us to sanity.

Step Two
Came to believe that a power greater than ourselves could restore us to sanity.

Came to believe—In the beginning, we came to believe by attending meetings and listening. We heard others as they described a relationship with a Higher Power. We noticed that those who maintained a regular connection with this Power experienced what we sought—RECOVERY. Because we were members of a Twelve-Step program, the form of this Power was left to each of us to discover. We became willing to entertain the possibility there was something that could do for us what we could not do for ourselves.

Restore us to sanity—With the help of others in the program, we began to look more clearly at our own behavior. We discovered a great truth in Step Two: that continuing to act in a self-destructive manner, no matter how well-meaning we believed we were, was insane. And once this behavior became compulsive, any belief we held that we could control it on our own was equally insane.

Becoming honest with ourselves was at times painful. The reward was magnificent. As we came to believe and embrace the simple and profound truth offered in this Step, the seed of humility produced by our admission of powerlessness in Step One was nurtured. We experienced a sense of freedom and hope by our willingness to have a true Higher Power. At this point our faith emerged.

excerpt from Step Two in the CoDA *Twelve Steps Handbook*

In Step One, we recognize our failure in our own attempts to play God. We also allow others to be our God. We recognize that we must seek help beyond ourselves and those to whom we've given authority. In doing so, we become ready to develop a belief in a power greater than ourselves—a power that can restore us to sanity and health.

In Step Two, we begin establishing or strengthening this belief. For those of us who do not know a Higher Power, we embark on a new and wondrous relationship. For those of us who have a relationship with a Higher Power, this Step can help us strengthen its weaker areas.

Through our work in the First Step, we learn that as children, we may have prayed often for God's help, but the neglect and/or abuse continued. The authority figures in our lives were often unavailable and absorbed in their own addictions and codependence. As adults, we try to leave those circumstances behind, only to find ourselves in adult relationships where similar or extreme opposite behaviors occur.

We keep praying to God, but nothing changes until we turn away from our addictions and from the people with whom we're obsessed. We may continue to look to others for solutions, peace, hope, and our sense of identity and worth. We begin to feel more worthless because our humanness won't allow us to be our own Higher Power or we give that power to others. We are left with few choices. Only one offers us the freedom, strength, and serenity we so desperately need.

Some of us come to CoDA already believing in a loving God. We may feel God's loving presence through hardship, or believe that God abandons us in times of need. Many times, shame causes us to believe we're not good enough to warrant God's love, goodness, or grace.

Some of us have little or no concept of a Higher Power, or we may have forgotten or abandoned our learned concept of God.

A review of Chapters One and Two can help us clarify our concept of a Higher Power. In our childhood, our Higher Power may have had personality traits similar to authority figures. At times, God may still resemble a punishing or shaming person like a tyrannical spiritual leader, family member, or friend. We find it helpful to list the personality characteristics and traits of a Higher Power with whom we do have or would like to have a relationship. This can help us determine if we have transferred personality traits and characteristics from our former or present abusers to our Higher Power. To better understand these concepts, we talk with others in CoDA and learn from their experiences. Some people choose nature, the universe, or their home groups of Co-Dependents Anonymous as their Higher

Power. Others choose, renew or strengthen a belief in a Higher Power of religious convictions. We learn how they struggle, just like us, and how they experience many miracles in their lives and relationships with God and others, often in spite of their doubts and fears. We learn of their spiritual discoveries and how God works in their lives, even when they ignore God's presence. We learn how their lives are restored through faith and even divine intervention, sometimes in the face of life threatening circumstances. For some people, placing faith and belief in a Higher Power may be difficult because it means letting go of illusionary safeguards. It means believing or being willing to believe that a power greater than ourselves can do for us what we're unable to do for ourselves.

We remember we're being asked in Step Two only to believe or be willing to believe that a power greater than ourselves can restore us to sanity. We're not required to believe in another person's personal God, religion, or spiritual concept. Our Higher Power must feel right and safe to us. Our Higher Power must be one of our own choosing and concept. As we begin placing our faith in this renewed or newly established relationship, we begin to feel relief and a new sense of hope. We no longer need to control or avoid ourselves or others. We begin placing this relationship first to gain the strength and peace necessary to maintain recovery and live life rather than survive life.

In Step Two, we experience a newfound faith and responsibility. Our Higher Power does not accomplish our recovery work for us; we must do our share. Every day, we must attempt to renew and strengthen our relationship with our Higher Power and share our newly fortified experience, strength, and hope with other codependents.

With the help of a loving Higher Power, we are now ready to begin Step Three.

Step Three
Made a decision to turn our will and our lives over to the care of God as we understood God.

> **Made a decision**—We had admitted our powerlessness over the compulsive behaviors we had practiced for so long. We were beginning to believe a Higher Power could relieve them. The next Step was obvious. If we believed we were powerless and that a Higher Power could transform us, why not accept it? Why not give God a chance where we had failed? Besides, what did we have to lose but our misery?
>
> **Our will and our lives**—Our old ideas called out to us to return to self-will. Once again, we attempted to play God in our lives and the lives of others. Old doubts sometimes challenged our new thinking. We began to believe that even though this program worked for others—we were different. Losing hope, we questioned our ability to change.
>
> It was this experience that led us to acknowledge that this program of recovery was not a "flash in the pan," something nice to do on a pleasant afternoon. It represented our opportunity to live as whole human beings. And if we wanted it, we would need the willingness to go to any lengths—even if it meant asking God for help more than once.

excerpt from Step Three in the
CoDA *Twelve Steps Handbook*

In this Step we continue to develop and strengthen our relationship with God.

We pause to read this Step and what it suggests we do. We reflect upon its wisdom and our feelings about surrender.

We are asked to make a decision to let go of ourselves and others. We decide whether we can trust in God to care for all we consider precious and important. Trust does not come easily for many of us. For years, we put our faith and hope in ourselves and others. We relied on everything but our Higher Power to provide us peace, happiness, and well-being.

Control and avoidance have demanded a great deal of our time, attention and energy. We know we've abandoned ourselves and given others power over our well-being. Some of us pray and hope that God will help. But until we let go on a heartfelt level, our codependence continues.

Through our work with Steps One and Two, we realize that our control and avoidances no longer work and that others are no longer responsible for our happiness and well-being. We realize how our playing God or giving the power of God to others is short-lived, painful, and, ultimately, self-destructive. We gain a better or new understanding of a power greater than ourselves. Until we turn our emotional attention to God, we are still bound by our codependent thoughts, feelings, and behaviors.

We may be frightened by the thought of allowing God to take care of us and the other people in our lives. What if God doesn't do what we think best? What if things don't go the way we would like? What if "they" don't change? What will happen if others don't like us as we change in recovery?

As codependents, our fears are understandable. They lie beneath our intense need to control and avoid ourselves and others. In letting go of control and avoidance, these fears often surface and we are emotionally faced with our spiritual dilemma. Once we face these fears, we are at a crossroads: Do we return to playing God in ours and others' lives or do we turn our will and life over to the care of God as we understand God?

We remember that we are asked only to make a decision. We are not asked to instantly experience total faith and trust in God. Our ability to trust in healthy ways has, more than likely, been negatively affected by the codependence in our lives. We cannot expect to make this decision without some reservation and fear.

To cope with our fears, we ask God for courage and strength. We seek the support and understanding of our sponsors and recovery friends. Some of us may create a special time and place to complete this Step. In any case, when we are ready, we may find this prayer to be helpful:

> *God, I give to You all that I am and all that I will be for Your healing and direction. Make new this day as I release all my worries and fears, knowing that You are by my side. Please help me to open myself to Your love, to allow Your love to heal my wounds, and to allow Your love to flow through me and from me to those around me. May Your will be done this day and always. Amen*

When we make this decision, our fears, concerns and reservations subside, and our relationship with God grows.

Our trust grows stronger by continuing our recovery work and experiencing how God helps us to change our codependent behavior. We feel a healthier sense of well-being. Our tendency to control and avoid others and ourselves decreases.

As we progressively release our control-and-avoidance behaviors and refocus our attention and energies on our own personal recovery, we're not as overwhelmed by life's circumstances. We experience a growing sense of serenity. We more effectively release the lives of others to the care of God, as well.

We may not realize how dramatic the changes have been in our lives and circumstances because they're so often subtle. They happen day-by-day, and we may not see them. A review of just how far we've progressed over the past month, six months, and year(s), can reassure us of God's continuing presence and care.

We may experience circumstances when we think God cannot or will not help. We may revert to our former codependent survival patterns. If we look closely, we find that fear, shame, or fear of shame are at work once again. We can walk a path toward serenity again by praying for God's help and guidance, talking with our sponsors and recovering friends, and reviewing these first three Steps.

Day by day we strengthen our relationship with God. We become more responsible for our recovery by placing this relationship first. Every day, we find it helpful to renew our decision to turn our will and our lives over to the care of God.

As we continue to do this, our trust in God grows. With our Higher Power's help, the program of CoDA and the care and support of our sponsors and recovery friends, we can strive for a life of balance, strength, and serenity.

Having brought an end to our spiritual dilemma, and having developed a growing trust in the loving care of God as we understand God, we are ready to begin the healing of our relationship with ourselves. Step Four begins this healing process.

Step Four
Made a searching and fearless moral inventory of ourselves.

Searching and fearless—Searching meant to look over carefully in order to find something lost or concealed; to come to know, to learn, to seek; to conduct a thorough investigation. And fearless meant courageous, bold, and unconquerable. If "searching" meant to look for something lost or concealed, we were really on the brink of a great adventure, the discovery of our true selves. But this word "fearless" was another story. Many of us still believed it was impossible to approach this process without fear. We were comforted by others who had felt as we had. We realized that we were not alone, that we were embarking upon this journey with God who would guide us gently along our way.

Moral inventory of ourselves—The first part of this Step defined the attitude we adopted as we worked it—one that was searching and fearless. The second part of Step Four gave us our focus and direction. This inventory would be only of ourselves, and it would pertain to our personal behavior in as many life experiences as we could recall. The word "moral" had many synonyms; among them were words like honest, straightforward, fair, and open. The message in Step Four was clear. This inventory of ourselves was to be honest and straightforward, not critical or abusive.

If this was to be a thorough inventory, we would need to list our assets and our liabilities. That meant we would have a truly balanced picture of ourselves. For some, it was more difficult to discover good points than to face shortcomings. For others, acknowledging positive qualities made the task less painful. Whatever our feelings were about this, we were encouraged to do both, as each was an important aspect of a thorough inventory.

excerpt from Step Four in the CoDA *Twelve Steps Handbook*

Until now, we've focused on establishing or renewing our relationship with God as we understand God. In Step Four, we begin a spiritual journey of healing our relationship with ourselves.

Many beliefs, religions, and philosophies speak of cleansing the soul to spiritually evolve. Just as we boil river water to remove impurities for drink, so must we go through this process to drink more fully from life. As we do, we're better able to separate and appreciate our goodness from our unhealthy thoughts and behaviors.

Our cleansing begins with an honest and thorough self-assessment through the work of Step Four. We look to this Step to continue our process of freedom and to help us become all that God intends us to be.

Step Four may appear overwhelming because it often causes memories to surface, particularly memories with feelings of pain, shame, and guilt that we tried to avoid. We review our first three Steps. We remember our powerlessness and unmanage-ability. We think about the strength and hope we experience in our relationship with our Higher Power. We look to our sponsors and others in CoDA for their support and guidance. We know we're not alone. Many before us have completed this Step. We rely on God to lead us on this difficult inward journey.

We remember that our courage to complete this Step doesn't come from the absence of fear but our willingness to walk through it. We work toward understanding our strengths and weaknesses, our internal assets and liabilities, who we are and what we've become as a result of our codependence. We look for understanding, not fuel to fire self-condemnation.

This Step is part of our healing—a form of emotional surgery that requires gentleness and care. We find it helpful to refer to Step Four in the CoDA *Twelve Steps Handbook* for insight, and to seek the support, guidance and experience of our sponsors and recovery friends.

A variety of methods are available to complete Step Four. One method is diagrammed on pages 46 & 47. In reviewing our lives, both the past and present, we list those people who have been affected by our codependent behaviors. We include God, ourselves, our mates, children, friends, family members, co-workers and people who participate in our various activities. In a second column, we list our codependent behaviors with each person throughout each relationship. Specific behaviors may be difficult to remember. This is defined in five areas: emotional, physical, sexual, spiritual and intellectual. Our behaviors could have included these:

Lying	Distancing
Manipulating	Punishing
Avoiding	Discounting
Denying	Offending
Passiveness	Bitterness
Aggressiveness	Abusing
Resenting	Enmeshing
Raging	Hypervigilence
Silence	Overcontrolling
Victimizing	Overpleasing
Abandoning	Teasing
Judging	Helplessness
Neglecting	Shaming
	Hating

The list above is not inclusive; we offer it as a beginning for exploration. To be honest and thorough we must ask ourselves if we've treated God, ourselves and others in these ways. Have we abused, abandoned, become enmeshed with, or neglected God, ourselves or others emotionally, physically, sexually, spiritually or intellectually? Because we may have reacted or responded to mistreatment by others, it's easy to rationalize or justify some of our codependent behaviors. Doing this only serves to maintain and continue these behaviors, and doesn't cause us to become accountable and responsible for changing them. We then create a third column to gain insight into what feelings drove our codependent behaviors. A fourth column can help us determine the consequences of our codependent behaviors; to that person, ourselves and the relationship. And a final or fifth column can help us determine our feelings about our codependent behaviors, the feelings that drive them and their consequences. The following two pages are an example of such an outline.

Person	My codependent behaviors & reactions	My feelings that drove those behaviors	Consequences to the person, myself & the relationship	My feelings about my behaviors & consequences
Mother	I made up lies to get her to give me money when I was broke 3 different times.	Shame about being irresponsible for my own finances. Fear of her judgments of me. Fear and anger about having to be financially responsible and having to get help.	Abandonment and neglect of my own financial responsibilities kept me financially and emotionally dependent on her. Manipulated her to be financially responsible for me. Kept me in the child role in our relationship and not equal.	Sad, ashamed, guilty.
Father	Stayed resentful, angry and bitter about his sexual, verbal and physical abuses of me without seeking help or resolving these. (He would pretend that everything was fine when I was with him.) Etc.	Fear, anger and shame about facing these issues. Fear of being abused or abandoned by him if I told him I was in CoDA or therapy. Fear of being labeled crazy and of being the "bad guy" in the family.	Continued loss of love and intimacy with him. Risk of my kids acting out my emotional secrets about him. Abandoned and neglected my own feelings about this. Needed to use anger, resentment and bitterness to cover my hurt, fear, and shame about being abused. Didn't learn to stand up for myself either with him directly or in some healthy way to gain a sense of empowerment with abusive men.	Lonely, sad, ashamed, scared, angry.
Joan (wife)	She raged at me at the park and I stayed silent for a couple of days.	Fear and terror of her raging or abandoning me if I stood up to her. Fear she might look for someone else. Fear and anger that she would make me out to be the wrong one.	Abandoned and neglected my own feelings about this. Neglected myself and the relationship by not standing up for myself. Enabled her to continue raging. Controlled her through silence. Maintained lack of intimacy by punishing her with silence.	Lonely, sad, scared, ashamed, guilty.

Person	My codependent behaviors & reactions	My feelings that drove those behaviors	Consequences to the person, myself & the relationship	My feelings about my behaviors & consequences
Bonnie (Daughter)	A couple of days after Joan raged at me in the park, I raged and dumped all over Bonnie for not emptying the trash. Everything was fine between Joan and me after that!	Months of anger, resentment, pain and shame about Joan's ragings that I never shared with Joan or addressed at all.	I abandoned and neglected my feelings about Joan's behavior and raging. I reinforced the role for Bonnie as my emotional scapegoat. I drove Bonnie and I further apart. I reinforced fear and lack of trust in Bonnie toward me. I reinforced the message to Bonnie that raging is part of a relationship and is OK.	Sad, ashamed, guilty, scared.
Allen (Boss, Friend)	He told his co-workers about something confidential that I shared with him, and I became angry and called in sick the next day, so that I wouldn't have to face them.	Fear that I might be fired if I told him how angry I was. Fear of losing the friendship if I told him how angry I was. Fear of him reacting to me in front of my co-workers. Fear of being judged by him and any co-workers as being too sensitive. Pain that my friend broke my confidence.	I abandoned and neglected my own feelings. Loss of trust and integrity in myself to stand up for myself and in him. Loss of intimacy within my friendship of integrity within my friendship by not being honest. I reinforced the value that it's OK for people to violate my confidences.	Sad, lonely, angry, guilty, ashamed, scared.

As we progress in this work, we see our codependent patterns emerge. Many times we react to people in similar or extreme ways—just as we reacted to a parent or authority figure from our childhood. We often put another person's face on this individual, not allowing us to see their true selves. We unknowingly recreate similar or unhealthy and abusive patterns within our adult relationships. We must become responsible and accountable for these behaviors today even though we learned them from our childhood.

To thoroughly explore and understand the relationship we have with ourselves and to bring balance to the work of our Fourth Step, we must also explore our strengths, assets, and positive behaviors. For this purpose, it's helpful to return to the previous outline. We do so with the intent of making a new list of these people and identifying our positive, healthy, appropriate, and loving behaviors in our relationships with each one.

In this new list, we add individuals who did not experience our codependent behaviors—people who have experienced our strengths, assets and positive behaviors. It is helpful also to include a column for our feelings about our strengths, assets and positive behaviors in each relationship. We might also want to include a column to identify when we behaved in a healthier manner than we did previously, to show progress on our recovery journey.

Some of us find it difficult to identify these behaviors. It can be insightful to ask our sponsors, recovery friends, mates, and family members about our strengths and positive behaviors. With an open heart and mind, we must strive to listen to what they share. At times, it's easy to become downtrodden with shame and fear from our past. Just as a tablecloth covers the beauty of a fine oak table, shame and fear cover our ability to witness our own God-given beauty, talent and goodness.

When we look at our relationship with ourselves from a more balanced perspective, we begin to realize we're not bad people at all. The shame messages we learned about ourselves as children are untrue. This is the way many of us learned codependent behaviors.

We must remember not to use our strengths and positive behaviors to minimize our feelings about our codependency. We must maintain accountability and responsibility for these behaviors and our feelings about them in order to change them. Today, we're not victims. We can't blame people, places or things for our problems or codependent behaviors anymore.

We become more humble as we explore our relationship with ourselves through the work of Step Four. It helps us open the door to see, accept, and begin loving ourselves as we are. From this place of humility, we've become ready to complete Step Five.

Step Five
Admitted to God, to ourselves, and to another human being the exact nature of our wrongs.

> **Admitted to God, to ourselves, and to another human being**—At the suggestion of CoDA friends who had already worked these Steps, we decided to risk this exposure we feared in the safest possible way, with our Higher Power. By admitting first to God, we were reminding ourselves that the primary element in our recovery was spiritual.

Encouraged by other CoDA members, we stuck with this section of Step Five and, eventually, the pressing weight of what we had locked inside began to lift. This self-admission had become a vehicle for self-acceptance.

excerpt from Step Five in the
CoDA *Twelve Steps Handbook*

In Step Four, we began our cleansing process by becoming aware of ourselves and our codependent behavior and addictions. We struck and held a match to shed light on those aspects about ourselves we've been unable or unwilling to see.

In Step Five we continue our cleansing process. Becoming accountable to our Higher Powers, to ourselves, and to another person for our feelings, behaviors, and addictions is imperative to our recovery. Without accountability, our spiritual program is incomplete, and we continue to play God or give others that role.

Many of us experience strong feelings as we consider working this Step. Some of us fear sharing our inventory with another person, believing no one else could have been as bad. Some of us fear being criticized, judged or shamed for what we've done. Some of us want to defend and minimize our inventory, blaming others for our behaviors. Some of us fear how we might feel about ourselves as we share our inventory.

These fears are natural in completing our Fifth Step for the first time. Though we may have strong feelings in approaching this Step, many of us find that in sharing our strengths and weaknesses with God and another person, we experience newfound acceptance, humility and compassion for ourselves.

We find it helpful to give time and thought to finding the right person with whom we may complete Step Five. Is there someone with whom we feel safe sharing our secrets? Is there a person we can trust to maintain our confidences? Many of us complete our Fifth Step with our sponsors. Some of us share this Step with clergy, a spiritual advisor, or a therapist. In any case, it's important to complete our Fifth Step with someone outside our families who can be objective, loving, caring, and compassionate. We look for someone who has an understanding of codependence, its devastation and the recovery process.

In completing Step Five with the person we have chosen, we must remember we're allowing our Higher Power to cast a healing spiritual light on our darkness. We must be thorough and honest. Withholding aspects of our past continues to enslave us. By sharing our past with God, ourselves, and another human being, we may understand God always knows what we keep concealed or are unable to see. We learn how God never abandons us, but we do abandon ourselves.

Upon completing Step Five, we often gain an even deeper awareness and a healthy respect for our powerlessness and unmanageability. Many of us experience a great sense of relief and a new spiritual and emotional freedom from the bondage of our past. For some, this is immediate; for others, it is a gradual awakening as we continue our recovery journey.

We may feel a deeper gratitude for God's help and the recovery process. In quiet reflection, we become aware of our losses but we realize that only through God's grace have we come this far.

We're not ignorant anymore of who we are and what we've done. Enlightenment always brings responsibility. We must continue to strive to change our codependent thoughts and behaviors with our Higher Power's help.

We remember that this Step is not an instant cure for our past and present problems. We must continue our recovery journey and our cleansing process by strengthening our willingness through the work of Step Six.

Step Six
Were entirely ready to have God remove all these defects of character.

> **Entirely ready**—We were reminded that "entirely ready" meant completely prepared. Having completed our Fifth Step was a large part of that preparation. We examined this phrase more closely and found we could test it in our daily lives.
>
> The answer came to us, that all of our character defects were, in some way, products of our own self-will. They were survival tools from our past and, while they seemed to provide for our apparent well-being, they were no longer enough. We wanted to live, not merely survive, and for that we would need a clean slate.
>
> **To have God remove all these defects of character—** It was suggested that we view these shortcomings as a

protective shell that we had outgrown. Hanging onto them would be as self-defeating as a bird keeping some of its shell or a butterfly clinging to a bit of its cocoon. At this point in our recovery, our character defects didn't protect us at all. They were excess baggage that dragged us down, often blinding us to our potential.

**excerpt from Step Six in the
CoDA *Twelve Steps Handbook***

Step Six asks us to begin taking positive action toward changing those defects of character we outlined in our Fourth Step. It is a part of our cleansing process. Now we must apply the faith and trust we developed while working our Second and Third Steps and put them into greater action. In doing so, we take the decision of turning our will and our lives over to the care of God and advance one Step further by becoming willing and ready for God to remove all our defects of character.

Our defects of character may have served us well, even though they're destructive. By reviewing our Fourth Step outline, we can see the horrible consequences of holding onto them. We're left with little choice but to let these character defects go.

To complete Step Six, we question our readiness and willingness. Will we continue relying on our codependent behaviors to relate to God, ourselves and others? Or, do we accept the challenge of change in our lives?

Many of us question, "Do I have to become a saint?" "Do I have to work a perfect recovery program?" "How will I protect myself?" "What will I do?" In time, we learn that perfectionism is unachievable in this life and is a characteristic driven by a codependent past. Instead, we must devote ourselves to progress, with its ups and downs, in whatever stage of life we may be. We find it important to avoid using "progress" or "trying" as excuses or disguises for fear and an unwillingness to move forward.

For some of us, considering our readiness and willingness causes us to become fearful because we don't know how to behave in healthy ways. Some of us become resistant to change or fearful of losing our power.

In one way or another, our character defects emerge to provide us a sense of power—false as it is. To make the transition from self-powered/powerless individuals to healthier human beings requires the help of our Higher Power. Only our Higher Power can remove our defects of character that have provided us unhealthy defenses, protection and false power.

In exploring our readiness and willingness to complete Step Six, we find it helpful to once again share our thoughts and feelings in CoDA meetings, with our sponsors, and our recovery friends. Above all, we seek the help and guidance of our Higher Power through prayer and meditation. We remember again that courage doesn't come from the absence of fear but the willingness to walk through it. It is only through God's power that we make true and significant progress. At times, we may be barely willing to let go. Yet even the smallest amount of willingness opens the door to the power of God's healing.

Readiness and willingness are key attitudes in our process of experiencing change from our character defects. Our experience has shown that many defects may be removed by God without effort. Some may require our conscious attention and work with the guidance and support of God and our Fellowship. Some of our defects may be complicated and require the additional guidance of the professional community.

If we are entirely ready, or thoroughly prepared and willing to have God remove all our defects of character, then it's time to continue our positive actions and move to Step Seven.

Step Seven
Humbly asked God to remove our shortcomings.

> **Humbly asked God**—After much consideration, we defined humility as freedom from false pride and arrogance. True humility allowed us to see things as they were. We would not instruct our Higher Power to remove our shortcomings. Neither would we beg. Instead, we would gently, peacefully ask.
>
> **To remove our shortcomings**—Having asked God to remove our shortcomings, many of us experienced their loss with sadness. We had never expected to grieve for what we had come to believe was detrimental to our happiness. We began to see that these "old friends" had served us well. Like a childhood life preserver that no longer fit, we put them aside. With the help of God, we were learning to swim.
>
> **excerpt from Step Seven in the CoDA *Twelve Steps Handbook***

Step Seven helps us to complete our spiritual cleansing process in our relationship with ourselves. It opens our hearts even more deeply to a relationship with God.

Heartfelt humility is a vital part of this Step. Without it, there is little room for a Higher Power to work within us and through us. Step Seven helps us to acknowledge our imperfections. Each of us is different, but humility allows us to experience true spiritual equality with others.

In one way or another we each reach our unique "bottom" in our codependence. We feel a deep level of powerlessness. We learn that God can help us if we are willing to do our part in helping ourselves. We surrender to God's will for our lives. We open our eyes to the devastating effects of our codependent behaviors in all of our relationships. We share the exact depths of our codependence with God, ourselves and others. We recognize we have failed in our best attempts to participate in truly loving and intimate relationships with God, ourselves and others.

Each aspect of our Step work has brought us an ever-deepening understanding and experience of our humanness. Our heartfelt humility fuels our desire, readiness and willingness to have God remove our character defects. It is from this heartfelt and humble posture that we are ready to complete Step Seven.

In doing so, many of us search our hearts for the prayer and communication with God that express what we truly feel. Some of us find helpful the following prayer from Step Seven in the CoDA *Twelve Steps Handbook*:

> *In this moment, I ask my Higher Power to remove all of my shortcomings, relieving me of the burden of my past. In this moment, I place my hand in God's, trusting*

that the void I experience is being filled with my Higher Power's unconditional love for me and those in my life.

In completing Step Seven, we allow our Higher Power to guide our lives and the healing of our codependent behaviors. We begin to understand that our recovery can continue only through our Higher Power's love and care. We no longer play God or place others in that role. We become partners with our Higher Power. We ask for God's help as we apply healthy new behaviors in our relationships with God, ourselves and others.

Though we may behave in some of the same codependent ways, we become convinced, regardless of the timing and ways, that God will continue to remove these shortcomings. We ask God to remove them as they happen and seek additional help when necessary. We must try to be consistent in our readiness and our willingness. In doing so, our maturing, healthier selves will continue to emerge.

By completing these first seven Steps, we establish strong foundations in our relationships with God and with ourselves. We begin to experience choices in our lives. We become aware of our self-defeating thoughts and behaviors and begin replacing them with positive thoughts and healthy behaviors. We move farther from shame and fear to an even greater acceptance of ourselves and others. As this transformation continues, we notice a growing inner strength. People and situations that frightened, angered, overwhelmed, or overpowered us become less powerful. We develop self-acceptance and personal integrity.

With these greater strengths, it is time to begin the work of healing our relationships with others through Step Eight.

Step Eight
Made a list of all persons we had harmed, and became willing to make amends to them all.

Made a list—In the first half of Step Eight we were asked to list everyone who had been harmed by our personal unmanageability. Our name came first and the reason was obvious. We had been the least able to escape from our own codependence and, therefore, in most cases, we received the greatest injuries. A change in behavior toward ourselves would have to come first.

Nothing we could have possibly done as children ever warranted the abuse we'd received. What was important here was to discover if we had harmed ourselves or others as a way of venting our rage, grief, or hurt at these past injustices.

Became willing to make amends to them all—The purpose of Step Eight was to focus our attention on becoming ready to face those we had harmed. And it was in becoming willing that we got stuck. We wondered what action we could take to prepare ourselves for this new task.

This self-forgiveness would be instrumental in moving us out of our codependence and into healthy, whole relationships with God, ourselves, and our fellow human beings.

excerpt from Step Eight in the
CoDA *Twelve Steps Handbook*

To this point, we have made great strides in establishing or renewing and healing our relationships with God and ourselves. It's time to turn our attention and energy to healing our relationships with ourselves and others, both past and present. Step Eight helps us to prepare to be accountable to others in a direct and positive manner for our codependent behaviors.

Step Eight consists of two parts. First, we concentrate on making our list. Then, we focus on becoming willing to make amends.

As we make our list, we find it helpful to refer to our Fourth Step inventory. We review our inventory and highlight the names of all those whom we have harmed—including God and ourselves. We may think we can avoid highlighting some aspects of our inventory. After all, some people may not know we had harmed them. However, we find it important at this stage of our recovery work to include even the smallest inappropriate behavior. As in all our previous work, we need to be thoroughly honest with ourselves about those people we've hurt.

Because we were raised in families where abuse, abandonment, neglect, enmeshment, alcoholism, sex addiction, eating disorders, or any other addiction may have existed, we need to be clear about how these influences have affected our adult lives. Have we ignored our relationship with God or taken it for granted? Have we blamed God, ourselves, or others for our life experiences? Have we, as a result of emotional abuse, become critical and judgmental of ourselves or others? Have we, as a result of neglect, ignored our personal needs or those of our mates and children? Have we secretly held onto resentment, bitterness, or hatred toward those who had neglected, abused, or abandoned us in our childhood and adult life? Can we let go of fear and resentment as false power and establish healthy boundaries?

We must ask ourselves these types of questions as we prepare our list and discuss it with our sponsor. As we do, we may add more names. Once we feel we have thoroughly completed our list, we move on to the second half of Step Eight.

This part of the Step asks us to become willing to make amends. Once again, we have an opportunity to let go of our will or control and allow our Higher Power to guide us. We remember why we entered the program of Co-Dependents Anonymous. Most of us made a commitment to be willing to go to any lengths for our recovery. Making amends for our past wrongs is important and vital to this process.

In many cases we find willingness to be the most difficult part of this Step. It's natural to feel some fear as we consider our willingness to make amends; we're literally facing our codependent past head-on.

Some of us fear facing the members of our families of origin or people we have skillfully avoided for many years. Some of us fear how others will react to our amends. There are those of us who fear the consequences of our past codependent behaviors.

No matter how severe the consequences, we must be willing to address them all. We must be willing to become accountable in all areas of our lives: our spirituality, our families and friendships, as well as our sexual, social, business, financial, and legal lives. We must face the reasonable consequences of our codependent behaviors. We're not helpless victims or offenders anymore. Rationalizing, judging, procrastinating, explaining, avoiding, minimizing, and manipulating are now useless tools of our codependent past. They've been replaced with willingness and honesty.

Our emotional wounds and boundaries may require more work and healing before we are ready to complete this Step with some people on our list. Our willingness will come in time. We must commit, however, to healing these wounds and boundaries and to completing Steps Eight and Nine when we have the strength.

Our job is to list the exact nature of our wrongs, to accept and forgive ourselves for our wrongdoings, to be willing to make amends to those we have wronged, and to be willing to face the reasonable consequences for our actions. We leave the outcome of these efforts to God. We have come to trust in God's time and way that the outcome of our willingness and honesty always works for the benefit of all involved.

We remember that making amends is meaningless without the willingness and effort to change our codependent behaviors. Otherwise, we're simply putting a temporary bandage on the problem. Sooner or later the problem always returns.

In our efforts to complete this Step, we find invaluable the strength and support of our sponsor and recovery friends. Our sponsors are helpful in determining what, and in how much detail, to share with each person on our lists. We may practice our amends with our sponsor, whose experiences offer us hope and add to our willingness. Most importantly, we rely upon our Higher Power for the courage to maintain our willingness to make amends.

Through our self-forgiveness, and with our integrity and dignity humbly and spiritually fortified, we can address those whom we have harmed and attempt to make right our wrongs. We are ready to complete Step Nine.

Step Nine
Made direct amends to such people wherever possible, except when to do so would injure them or others.

> **Made direct amends… wherever possible**—And so we arrived at a method of making amends—to acknowledge our harmful behavior and the other person's feelings in the matter, and to follow that with a change in our own behavior.
>
> **Except when to do so would injure them or others**—We looked at this statement in several ways, and included ourselves in the word, "others."
>
> We could not afford to enter into this amends-giving with expectations of those to whom we owed amends. By doing so, we could be injuring ourselves with disappointment and possibly resentment.
>
> excerpt from Step Nine in the CoDA *Twelve Steps Handbook*

To complete our part in the healing of all our relationships, we must complete Step Nine. It is the work we had prepared ourselves for in Step Eight. We will have fallen short in our preparations if we approach Step Nine with any motivation other than to ask for God's highest good. We make amends only for the healing of our codependence, not to manipulate others in any way.

In addition, we risk failure if we approach this Step with expectations of how our amends will turn out. Some of us expect personal accountability first from those who have harmed us. We believe our pain will be relieved if other people make amends too. If our motives for our amends and changes are based on expectations that others will now like, forgive, accept or become available to us, we're likely to be deeply disappointed. Nor can we expect everything to go our way.

These expectations can vary from person to person and are usually rooted in fear—fear that the outcome will not be of our choosing. Just as we addressed our fears about possible consequences in Step Eight, we must clear our minds of our expectations, offer our fears to God, seek the support of the Fellowship, and ask for God's help in letting go.

When we approach each of our amends, we remember God is working through us, and we ask for our Higher Power's presence and guidance. We seek the help of our sponsors and recovery friends to determine the best possible attitude to serve God, others, and ourselves through our amends. We allow our Higher Power to be in control of our lives.

In making our direct amends, we recommend simple, direct, and specific communications. We approach God, ourselves, and others with compassion and understanding, maintaining our humility, spirituality, and boundaries to the best of our ability.

Our Higher Power has been there for us always. If our behaviors have been inappropriate toward God in our past, it is God to whom we owe our first amends. Some of us complete this Step with God through guidelines set forth by our religious and spiritual organizations. Some of us complete these amends by writing them in a letter and reading it to God in God's presence. When we do, it's important to make time for ourselves to meditate with God to experience God's love, care, and forgiveness.

Although there are many creative methods to approach our amends with God, the best way is to live progressively healthier and more loving lives.

If we have been codependent with others, we probably have been codependent with ourselves. Our next step is to make direct amends to ourselves for our self-abandonment, self-neglect, and self-abuse.

We may find it helpful to write a letter to ourselves outlining our inappropriate behaviors toward ourselves. We may imagine ourselves and/or our child selves in the room with us while we read our letter of amends. We may ask our sponsor to be there during this time. Or, we may create time to face ourselves in the mirror and, while making eye contact, share our wrongs and make our amends. However we decide to complete this Step with ourselves, it is important to begin treating ourselves with love, respect, and care.

Next, we approach all others on our list. We find it helpful to first tell them how we have reached this point in our lives and recovery. We then share our wrongs and make our amends. It is not a time to argue, debate, criticize, or judge others. We leave judgments to God. As we outline our inappropriate behaviors and amends, other people may react angrily. They may be hurt or understanding. Our job is to listen and acknowledge their feelings.

A simple formula and guideline for completing each amend is found in Step Nine in the CoDA *Twelve Steps Handbook*:

> *"...to acknowledge our harmful behavior and the other person's feelings in the matter and to follow that with a change in our own behavior."*

We recommend that we share what we are specifically doing to change our behavior. Over time, as our behaviors match our words, the people we have harmed will come to trust us more fully.

Some people may see our codependent behaviors as normal and want to discount them and our amends. Accepting this lack of insight, and reaffirming our wrongs and amends, helps us to keep our boundaries and recovery perspective in order. We remember we are cleaning up our part in each relationship, no matter how others may see the situation.

Some people to whom we owe amends may not be living or can't be found. Writing letters and reading them to God and our sponsor helps us to complete this Step. We remain prepared, however, for the opportunity to complete this Step with those we can't find, should the opportunity present itself in the future.

Some of our wrongdoings may involve financial restitution, legal or business issues, emotional or sexual problems, or other sensitive areas. These amends may require investigation first. Talking with our sponsor and recovery friends, and seeking the guidance of spiritual, legal, therapeutic and other professional communities can be extremely helpful in determining the best possible approach to each amend.

We also need to recognize there are some doors that are better left closed. Though we may be willing, some people and their families would be further injured in our amends-making process. Asking our Higher Power for discernment and discussing each situation with our sponsor and recovery friends will usually lead us to appropriate decisions.

When there is no possibility of making direct amends, being of service to others is our amends. In giving, we receive. Through God's grace, and in gratefully offering our service to others, we gain peace in a spirit once filled with remorse and pain.

With the help of God and the CoDA Fellowship, we complete our Ninth Step and free ourselves of the laborious burden of our codependence. Our relationships with God and ourselves stand on new firm ground, even more spiritually empowered and free. In time, many of our relationships with others heal. True acceptance and forgiveness become sound precepts in our approach to life.

Our greater challenge now is to work consistently toward changing and improving ourselves as human beings. By applying our willingness to this challenge, we are ready to incorporate Steps Ten, Eleven, and Twelve into our daily recovery program.

Step Ten
Continued to take personal inventory and when we were wrong, promptly admitted it.

Continued to take personal inventory—There were times it seemed we were being nagged by feelings of fear, rage, hurt, or shame with no clear explanation. During these situations, we put the first three Steps into action. We acknowledged our powerlessness over this condition and affirmed our belief in God's power to bring us to balance. Then, we asked our Higher Power to reveal what we needed to know about the situation. Usually the answer came, and we could take whatever action we thought was appropriate. If it seemed slow in coming, we asked for patience and faith.

And when we were wrong, promptly admitted it—Step Ten seemed to suggest that we had made some progress, that we had become capable of handling our lives with even greater maturity than we believed possible. "When we were wrong," reminded us that not every unpleasant situation was our doing. It suggested we could cultivate the willingness to admit our wrongs when the fault was ours and the courage to set boundaries when the fault lay elsewhere.

> excerpt from Step Ten in the
> CoDA *Twelve Steps Handbook*

As part of our daily maintenance program, practicing Step Ten helps us to maintain daily accountability, health, and continued growth in all areas.

Steps One through Nine helped us to heal our relationships with God, ourselves, and others. We shifted the focus from ourselves and others to God. Spiritual empowerment is now our mainstay. We no longer live one-up, one-down lives. We strive to change our unhealthy, inappropriate behaviors, and Step Ten helps us to remain focused on that goal.

This Step offers us not only consistency, but also continued progress in our present relationships. Continuing to take our personal inventory keeps us ready to change our codependent behaviors. Some of our habits are ingrained. Our goal, however, is to make consistent progress. We look for familiar codependent behaviors and areas where our boundaries with others need strengthening.

For many of us, a daily journal is a practical tool for this work. A journal becomes a record of our progress, growth and areas of our personality that still need attention.

At the end of the day and with our journal in hand, we take time for reflection. Some of us say a short prayer, asking God to reveal everything we should know about ourselves from this day. With gratitude, we review events from the past 24 hours. Though this Step is intended to focus on our wrongs, we find it helpful to give some attention to our assets and accomplishments in growth and recovery, as well.

We ask ourselves if we've remembered to check in with our Higher Power periodically. Are we able to maintain gratitude to God for all that has been given us this day?

Have we been short with our co-workers or families after a long day at work? Have we been feeling sorry for ourselves or isolated from others? Did we rage, overreact, or passively abuse someone? Did we take on others' feelings or responsibilities? Have we been controlled or manipulated by people, not said anything, and then resented them?

These and similar questions help us to take an honest daily look at our codependent behaviors and feelings toward God, ourselves, and others. We look to see if we have been building fear, shame, or resentments toward others. Have we abandoned, abused, or neglected ourselves in any way?

Once we're sure we have been honest and thorough in completing our inventory, we remember not to shame ourselves, but to be gentle. To shame ourselves would be indulging, once again, in our own self-abuse.

We determine what amends we need to make and the most appropriate ways to accomplish this. We remember to include any amends to God and ourselves. If we're unsure of the healthiest way to approach a situation, we share the circumstances with our sponsor and recovery friends.

Promptness is very important in completing this Step. If we procrastinate, we run the risk of not following through at all. Knowing what we need to do for ourselves and neglecting it becomes a form of self-abuse. To progress, we must continue working.

Because promptness is so important, we make any amends we owe God and ourselves each evening as we take our inventory. We ask, as well, for God's help and grace to accept and forgive ourselves, and for God's strength and courage to correct our wrongs and change our behaviors.

Over time, we find it helpful to review our journal. As we do, some of us may see consistent areas where we avoid responsibility and accountability in our relationships with God, ourselves, and others. Often these are areas where we hold greater fear, shame, and resentments. A review of the values and willingness we established in Steps Eight and Nine will help provide healthier solutions with these concerns.

At times, our resistance may be greater than the strengths we gained from working Steps Eight and Nine. We may be bucking against strongly rooted protective defenses from our childhood. Talking with our sponsor and recovery friends can help determine if the person or situation may be triggering deeper, unresolved feelings and patterns about people or situations from our past.

In these circumstances, and with other strongly held codependent patterns, repeating Steps One through Nine is our next alternative. In some areas where we seem to find no resolve at all, the professional community can offer support and guidance. Many of us find it helpful to balance professional support with our strengthening spiritual life.

As we continue to practice Step Ten in our daily lives, we gradually apply it to our experiences throughout the day. In our growing awareness, we learn to see our wrongful behaviors as they happen. Asking for God's assistance, we make our amends immediately and make note of healthier behaviors for similar situations in the future.

We develop an instinctive sense of when to set boundaries with others. With boundaries in place, we are less likely to passively or aggressively react to others; take on others' feelings, attitudes, or realities; or give away our own sense of self.

As a result, the remnants of our self-centered codependence start to disappear. We begin to accept and forgive ourselves and others more naturally. We become better equipped to experience more loving, intimate relationships with ourselves and those around us.

Having added the daily practice of accountability through Step Ten to our recovery program, it's time to expand our relationship with our Higher Power through Step Eleven.

Step Eleven
Sought through prayer and meditation to improve our conscious contact with God as we understood God, praying only for knowledge of God's will for us and the power to carry that out.

Sought through prayer and meditation to improve our conscious contact with God as we understood God—In the beginning, some of us needed direction. We weren't clear where prayer left off and meditation began. It was explained to us that prayer was talking to God. Meditation was listening for God's guidance.

How we chose to meditate and pray would be an individual decision. Because our conscious contact with God would be continually improving, our methods might change as we grew spiritually.

Praying only for knowledge of God's will for us and the power to carry that out—Just as each of us had to take our own inventory, request that our own character defects be removed, and make our own amends, so we learned that the purpose of the Eleventh Step suggested we improve our own bond with God.

excerpt from Step Eleven in the
CoDA *Twelve Steps Handbook*

Step Eleven guides us as we grow and evolve in our spiritual program. Remembering that codependence is a spiritual dilemma is crucial to our recovery. Through our codependent behaviors, we made people, places, and things our gods, giving them importance and power. To avoid the possibility of returning to our former codependent ways, we must pursue a greater relationship with our Higher Power on a daily basis.

By the time we reach Step Eleven, many of us have learned or reaffirmed that we are not alone. We may never have experienced a relationship with God or we may have avoided our Higher Power through our codependence, but God has always been there for us.

Throughout our Step work, we have been renewing or establishing a relationship with God. As in any fulfilling relationship, if we want a strong and healthy relationship with God, we must devote time and attention to it. We find this is best accomplished through daily prayer and meditation.

For some of us, praying on a daily basis is a new experience. Some of us have many years of practice. Before recovery, many of us who prayed often wondered why things weren't changing or were getting worse. The answer is obvious. Either we weren't listening for answers, or we were unwilling to carry out the answers we were given.

Most of us understand prayer simply to be our way of communicating with God. Some of us follow the guidelines and specific prayers of our religious and spiritual organizations. Those of us who have no religious affiliations may find help from the experiences shared by our sponsor and recovery friends.

If we are still unsure how to pray effectively, asking God directly to teach us will surely bring us what we need. As with all learned things, if we speak from the heart and practice daily, we will develop our own personal, unique, and effective communication with God.

If we previously expressed our codependence in our communications with others, it is reasonable to think we would continue these behaviors in communicating with God now and then. As subtle as codependence can be, we must be on guard for this even in our prayers.

Praying only for God's will for us may be difficult. It means we must be willing to let go of others and trust the outcome for their lives and ours to God.

Some of us, often without noticing, try to control the outcome of situations in our lives and others' through our prayers, because of our fears or other feelings. We have learned in recovery that we aren't in charge of others' lives nor will we benefit from trying to control God's will. To continue on our spiritual path, we must release our control to God.

Each of us is different; we come from varying backgrounds and have distinct life circumstances. God's will for one may not be the same as God's will for another. When we seem led to pray for others, asking for God's love, will, and the highest good is usually sufficient. Our lives become much simpler when we emotionally and spiritually let go, pray only for God's will for us, the power to carry that out, ask God to guide us and direct us throughout our day, and trust the outcome of ours and others' circumstances to our Higher Power's care.

In our relationship with God, meditation is our way of listening for God's will and experiencing God's presence. Some say we pray through our words; we listen with our hearts. To hear with our hearts, we must step out of our fast-paced, daily activities; quiet ourselves; and focus our attention on God as we understand God. To aid the quieting of our internal dialogues, some of us use music. Some of us rely upon physical and mental disciplines. And some of us simply sit quietly, close our eyes, and allow our thoughts to rest.

There are many forms of meditation. Finding one that fulfills our needs may take a little time. Whatever the form, it's important to allow ourselves to feel a heartfelt and spiritual connectedness with our Higher Power.

By meditating and/or praying daily to improve our conscious contact with God, we become more aware of God's presence in all aspects of our lives. We begin to see and hear answers to our prayers through surprising sources. It may happen directly in our meditation or prayer. At times, we may find answers we never prayed for, nor ever imagined.

Though we may have set aside specific times in the morning or evening to practice this Step, we also find that checking in with our Higher Power throughout the day helps us to improve our conscious contact with God. We might utter a prayer of gratitude for something that just happened or ask God's assistance when we're unsure of which path to take. We may even take time during a break or lunch to quietly meditate and renew our connection with God's presence.

In seeking God's will for us for specific situations, we may be led to let go emotionally and do nothing—neither taking nor making changes in our circumstances. When we are unsure of the right path, we review the possibilities with our sponsor and recovery friends. Often a different perspective sheds light on God's will for us.

Once we are assured of God's will, we ask for God's grace, strength, and courage to carry it out. This is especially important when circumstances are emotionally overwhelming. We must remember that God's power is always present for us. With daily application of this Step, we come to believe that the power of God always carries us through wherever God's will leads us.

As we grow through our daily practice of Step Eleven, we are truly allowing God to control our daily lives and recovery. Our fears decrease and we come to trust that all we need to meet each day is provided for by our Higher Power. Our strength and spiritual empowerment grow more present in all our relationships. Our faith in God is continually renewed as we watch God's miracles unfold in our lives. Our spirit progressively comes to know peace and well-being.

With our daily practice of trusting and strengthening our relationship with God in place, it is time to begin passing on to others all that we have been given in our recovery. Step Twelve shows us the way.

Step Twelve

Having had a spiritual awakening as the result of these steps, we tried to carry this message to other codependents, and to practice these principles in all our affairs.

Having had a spiritual awakening as the result of these steps—The first words of this Step were often glossed over in our eagerness to "carry the message." Upon reflection, however, we could see that these words described the very foundation of our recovery. We came to understand that as a result of putting the Twelve Steps to work in our lives, we were transformed and that no matter what we believed about ourselves, as long as we put these Steps into action, the result would be our spiritual awakening.

We tried to carry this message to other codependents— By living this program, one day at a time, we became the message we had hoped to carry. We shared our experience, strength and hope with other codependents at CoDA meetings or when asked.

It was our process, what we did, rather than our personality, that was the message. The way we "carried it" was by being where we could share it—with other people.

And practice these principles in all our affairs— The final phrase in this Step reminded us that we could not separate our spirituality from the rest of our lives. The principles embodied in the Twelve Steps and Twelve Traditions were not the private domain of CoDA meeting rooms. They were meant to be practiced in ALL our affairs.

excerpt from Step Twelve in the CoDA *Twelve Steps Handbook*

Many of us come to our first meeting of Co-Dependents Anonymous with the hope that we can find help. We hear other CoDA members talk about their experience, strength, and hope in working the Steps. We see the transformation that has happened in their lives and hear how they handle situations now that previously paralyzed them. We hear of their trust in their Higher Power, how they walk through their fears, hurts and anger, believing that God will see them through.

We hear of the spiritual principles found in CoDA and how CoDA is a spiritual program. Some of us wonder what they mean by spiritual principles and spiritual program. Not realizing it, we are about to embark on a journey of spiritual transformation. Now eleven Steps and a million miles later, we're embracing Step Twelve of the program of Co-Dependents Anonymous. In completing these Twelve Steps, we come to understand the meaning of spirituality in our lives.

Some say spirituality is how we allow our Higher Power to be expressed through us. Some say it is an expression of our own spiritual nature. Through our recovery, many of us believe it is both. However we define it, we now know it is a vital power which has helped us to sustain life, to heal, to become, and to become healthy human beings.

Each of us experiences spiritual awakenings by completing the first eleven Steps. Some of us call it "change in progress." Each step of the way, the spiritual doors of our being open more, and we experience a conscious awakening and greater awareness of God, our own spirit, and spiritual nature. It is the process of enlightenment, illuminating the greater truths of life, God, and God's way.

As a result, we become more consciously aware of ourselves and the physical life in which we live. We see God and our spiritual way of life with all its dimensions through new and different eyes. We understand living, codependence, and recovery with greater spiritual depth and wisdom.

If we had been searching for a spiritual awakening, we probably wouldn't have found it; it is a by-product of our work. As we concentrate on our immediate task of living our life day to day, we trust that God will continue healing and changing our spirit.

Spiritual awakening brings greater responsibility. Through our Step work, we gain a greater ability to respond to life, with its joys and difficulties, in more spiritually sound, mature, and healthy ways. Part of our greater responsibility includes carrying the message of hope of recovery to other codependents.

Throughout our recovery, God has continued to touch our lives through others. We have received a great gift. If we want to keep what we have been given, we must be willing to let go and give it away. We are a vessel for God's love and healing energy. We must try to pour out our gift of recovery and pass it on to others. We become the message, the experience, strength, and hope of recovery. Through our own enlightenment, we become God's light—a beacon for those who still suffer.

Service work is what we call giving what's been given to us. Someone else in CoDA may have reached out to us long before we became a member. Someone else paid the rent, opened the door, made coffee, and prepared the meeting room. Many people share their experience, strength, and hope through sponsorship, individual sharing, and in meetings. They have touched our hearts in many ways. Many have been of service in CoDA organizational work so that CoDA continues to be available to us. Each experience is a way of carrying the message.

In applying this Step to our recovery program, we see it is time to decide how we will carry the message of recovery to others. We determine in what ways we'll pass on what we have been given.

It's important to explore our feelings about being of service. Do we avoid this part of the program? Do we tend to jump in when others won't? Do we attempt to use this part of our program to exercise a desire to be in control or find ourselves trying to "fix" others? If our motives in this area are codependent-bound, practicing these principles in all our affairs is our guide to a greater purpose in carrying our message.

We carry our message to other codependents in many ways. First and foremost, we do so through the attraction that we provide by practicing these principles in all our affairs. We offer ourselves to whatever level of service work we seem led—from the individual CoDA meeting to CoDA's international organization. Whenever possible, we offer no hesitation when asked to chair a meeting, to share our experience, strength and hope, or to help organize a meeting or other CoDA event. Organizational service work is so important that the next chapter of this book is devoted to this message.

In other areas, we make ourselves available. When appropriate, we reach out to both the newcomer and experienced member with understanding, compassion, and care. We share our joys and triumphs, struggles and hurts, experiences and hopes of recovery.

When it is right for us, we make ourselves available in sponsorship to others. Our own sponsor and recovery friends can help us with this decision. There is no greater satisfaction than seeing God working through us to support the recovery of other codependents and watching them become all that God intended.

Both inside and outside of CoDA, we find no need for promotion, banners, or streamers. Like a bee naturally drawn to honey, the quiet humility of our experience, strength, and hope usually draws the newcomer, experienced member, and non-member who may need what we have been given. Our job is to share our story with them, invite them to a meeting, and be available to them in healthy ways.

As we continue to give to others what God has given to us, we continue to receive greater gifts. Our recovery becomes an exciting and rewarding journey of spiritual fulfillment. We gain a balance of all life's experiences, from joy and delight to sorrow and loss. We no longer live life in the extremes. We allow ourselves to become more open to God's continuing miracles and spiritual transformation.

We are about to complete the Twelve Steps of Co-Dependents Anonymous. With gratitude, we recognize God's love, healing, and guidance throughout our journey. We should pat ourselves on the back for our recovery efforts. But we are not finished; we are just beginning. We must continue to practice these principles in all our affairs. It is a lifelong process.

We must continue to apply the Steps and the spiritual principles found in Co-Dependents Anonymous throughout our daily lives and in all our relationships.

When our well-being is directly and negatively affected by a person or situation, we must admit, at that moment, we are powerless once again. Momentarily, our lives have become unmanageable. Whether formally applying the Steps or applying the principles found in the Steps to the moment, the Steps always show us the way.

We may never be free of our codependence. Remember, we are human and progress, not perfection, is our goal. We are not alone. God is always with us. We are joined in this journey by thousands of others. Individually and together, we express the spirit of recovery from codependence.

CoDA offers us a guide for living healthy and happy lives. By completing these Twelve Steps, again and again, and practicing these principles in all our affairs, we experience a new freedom from our self-defeating lifestyles and find a new strength to be what God intended—precious and free.

The Journey Continues

Our program of recovery is meant to be taken seriously, but we find balancing our recovery work with play, laughter, and fun is also important in our daily lives. These are some of God's most healing medicines. Rest, productivity, recreation, and exercise require our attention, as well. The benefits of these, we think, are obvious.

Responding to all our needs in healthy ways is an important part of our program for living. For some of us, responding to various needs may require time and practice. Eventually we become skilled in these areas.

As we progress in meeting our needs and sincerely continue our recovery program, our lives take on a well-rounded balance. This is the balance many of us have sought most of our lives.

Through God's abundant love, the spiritual principles of our program and our willingness to be rigorously honest in continuing our recovery to the best of our ability, we will come to know a new sense of belonging. We will begin to trust and believe in ourselves and that the healing of our past is possible. We'll no longer be controlled by fear and shame. We will find we are able to respond to life's challenges with courage, integrity, and dignity. Others will no longer be our gods. We will experience a new love and acceptance of ourselves and others. We will become capable of developing and maintaining healthy and loving relationships, and we will learn to see ourselves as equal to others. We will learn that it's possible for our families to mend and become more loving and intimate. We will come to know that we are each a unique creation of a loving Higher Power, born with beauty, value, and worth. And, we will progressively experience spiritual strength and serenity in our daily lives.

Some of us question if all this is just too much to hope for. Many of us on this journey do experience the fulfillment of these promises in our lives if we work each of the Steps to the best of our ability, particularly Steps Eight and Nine when we make amends to ourselves and other people we have harmed. We find further hope for our recovery in the promises stated on pages 83 and 84 of the book of *Alcoholics Anonymous* (reprinted with permission). These promises are being fulfilled daily by many recovering alcoholics and codependents.

They are:

> *We are going to know a new freedom and a new happiness. We will not regret the past nor wish to shut the door on it. We will comprehend the word serenity and we will know peace. No matter how far down the scale we have gone, we will see how our experience can benefit others. That feeling of uselessness and self-pity will disappear. We will lose interest in selfish things and gain interest in our fellows. Self-seeking will slip away. Our whole attitude and outlook upon life will change. Fear of people and of economic insecurity will leave us. We will intuitively know how to handle situations which used to baffle us. We will suddenly realize that God is doing for us what we could not do for ourselves. Are these extravagant promises? We think not. They are being fulfilled among us—sometimes quickly, sometimes slowly. They will always materialize if we work for them.*

In CoDA, spiritual transformation is our way of life. Being human, we make mistakes. We may have codependent slips from time to time. Remembering this, we approach recovery with love, acceptance, compassion, and care for ourselves and others. We remember that love and codependence cannot coexist. Progress is our goal. We give ourselves to God and ask to be guided throughout every moment of our day. We work our program to the best of our ability and help others to recover.

In this way, we are the experience, strength, and hope of recovery in Co-Dependents Anonymous.

CHAPTER FOUR

Service To Others

THE TWELVE TRADITIONS OF CO-DEPENDENTS ANONYMOUS

1. Our common welfare should come first; personal recovery depends upon CoDA unity.

2. For our group purpose there is but one ultimate authority—a loving Higher Power as expressed to our group conscience. Our leaders are but trusted servants; they do not govern.

3. The only requirement for membership in CoDA is a desire for healthy and loving relationships.

4. Each group should remain autonomous except in matters affecting other groups or CoDA as a whole.

5. Each group has but one primary purpose—to carry its message to other codependents who still suffer.

6. A CoDA group ought never endorse, finance or lend the CoDA name to any related facility or outside enterprise, lest problems of money, property and prestige divert us from our primary spiritual aim.

7. Every CoDA group ought to be fully self-supporting, declining outside contributions.

8. Co-Dependents Anonymous should remain forever nonprofessional, but our service centers may employ special workers.

9. CoDA, as such, ought never be organized; but we may create service boards or committees directly responsible to those they serve.

10. CoDA has no opinion on outside issues; hence the CoDA name ought never be drawn into public controversy.

11. Our public relations policy is based on attraction rather than promotion; we need always maintain personal anonymity at the level of press, radio and films.

12. Anonymity is the spiritual foundation of all our Traditions, ever reminding us to place principles before personalities.

Many members of the CoDA Fellowship have enhanced their understanding of the Twelve Traditions by working through *The Twelve Steps & Twelve Traditions Workbook of Co-Dependents Anonymous*. This can be done individually, with a sponsor, or in a study group meeting with other recovering codependents.

What is service work?

Our Twelve Steps and their spiritual principles help us to establish our recovery in our relationships with God, ourselves and others. They offer us spiritual guidelines to help us work with others. Service work in CoDA enables us to put these spiritual guidelines into practice. It embraces a healthy spirit of giving and enables CoDA to exist. Through service work, we acknowledge and esteem every person and their recovery, talents and abilities. Service work enables us to deepen the recovery we experience and allows God's gift of recovery to touch the hearts and minds of other codependents.

Each of us in CoDA has a variety of talents and skills to offer. CoDA offers a variety of service opportunities, from sponsorship and interactions with CoDA friends to group participation at local, regional, national, and international levels.

Determining our participation in service work is an individual decision. Once we choose the activity or role, we become open to another dimension of our recovery. As we review service opportunities and talk with our sponsor and recovery friends about various areas of service, we experience ourselves becoming a part of CoDA's spirit of giving. It's this spirit that assists CoDA members to work together for the good of CoDA in all of its areas of needs. Some of us may know exactly what service work we wish to pursue. Some of us may be unsure if we should do service work at all. We may feel overloaded with activities from our daily lives, not wanting to add on one more responsibility. Some of us may find it difficult working with others if we're not in charge, or we may feel we have nothing to offer. Whatever the case, each of us has a talent to share or an opportunity to give of ourselves. When we do, we grow in our recovery even more. No gift of service is better or less than others. They all have equal value—from setting up chairs for a CoDA meeting to participating in the CoDA Service Conference. Without all of us participating and giving of ourselves in some way through service work, CoDA cannot survive.

Our Traditions tell us that CoDA is self-supporting through our own contributions. We may think this Tradition refers to financial resources only; however, it includes our talents, ideas, abilities, time and care. The more we attend CoDA meetings, the more aware we become of the services provided by our membership. Pamphlets and newsletters for our local groups are paid by members' donations. These materials are written by members of CoDA who donate their time. Secretaries and treasurers of local CoDA groups prepare reports and handle expenses such as rent, anniversary chips, and literature. Community offices and committees are operated and supported by CoDA members to help coordinate CoDA efforts in local areas. One of the ways we celebrate our recovery with other CoDA members is by attending local, regional, national, and international conventions, all of which have been created, facilitated and supported by volunteer members and their contributions. With each passing day, CoDA benefits from the service work of others. The following are examples of areas in CoDA in which we may consider providing service:

- Sponsorship.
- Providing information on meeting times and locations.
- Listening to others.
- Starting a new meeting.
- Preparing chairs, literature, and refreshments for a meeting.
- Chairing a meeting.
- Greeting a newcomer.
- Cleaning up after a meeting.
- Volunteering as secretary or treasurer of a home group.
- Leading a meeting.
- Helping with CoDA workshops or social events.
- Updating meeting lists.
- Spreading the message of recovery to those who still suffer.
- Participating in a hospital or institutions meeting.
- Offering financial support through the Seventh Tradition.
- Establishing a Community Service Office.
- Starting or assisting with a local or regional newsletter.
- Working with local, regional, national, or international service offices.

- Writing articles and providing services for the Co-NNections newsmagazine.

- Volunteering for local, regional, national, or international conference and convention preparations.

- Improving the communication channels between local, regional, national, and international levels.

- Participating in committee work for local, regional, national, and international committees, such as Outreach, Hospitals and Institutions, Issues Mediation, Service Structure, Finance, Literature, Co-NNections, CoDA event committees, and others.

- Volunteering as a group representative, community representative, Voting Entity delegate, or CoDA, Inc. Trustee.

- Practicing and upholding the Traditions.

- Appropriately addressing Traditions violations.

Some may view this list as overwhelming, but when each of us contributes just a little to service work, we can accomplish so much together.

As we embark on the path of service work, we soon discover its benefits to CoDA, its members, and our personal recovery. We enhance our recovery to practice loving and healthy behaviors with those we join in service. We see the benefits of healthy reliance upon one another. We learn to accept our differences and similarities. We come to recognize that each of us has a purpose and path, all deserving of love and respect.

Codependence and service work

In our codependence, some of us use service work and other CoDA activities as a way to gain our value, worth, and identity. We satisfy our hunger for an identity, or to feel needed, by becoming overinvolved in our families, relatives, friends, careers, and other activities—many times to the detriment of our own needs. We literally give until it hurts our well-being.

Some of us isolate or avoid being available to others, fearful of our abilities or the judgments of others. Some of us are working to replace our controlling behaviors with healthy ones. Balance and workaholism are other issues with which many of us struggle. "How do we devote our time and talent in service work in healthy ways?" we ask.

Our answer is simple. Our Twelfth Step suggests we practice these principles in all our affairs. It doesn't matter if our codependence focuses on fixing, controlling, avoiding, or isolating. We can experience more personal recovery through service work by applying our recovery tools. Service work is a safe place to practice our recovery. It can become a mirror that reflects which areas of our personality may need refinement or change.

Each of us involved in service work in the CoDA Fellowship addresses our own recovery concerns at some point. It's a wonderful opportunity for growth. Service work allows us opportunities to practice setting boundaries, working with and accepting others, refraining from behaving in self-defeating ways, and developing healthy and loving relationships with other recovering codependents. It also helps us to become more sensitive to differences between caregiving and caretaking, responding and reacting, becoming a human being versus a human-doing.

At times, we place high expectations on the service work we provide, only to feel disappointed or disillusioned. At this extreme, we may vow never to do service work again. This is a terrible loss. By addressing our unrealistic expectations, we can expand our growth and recovery. Our groups can experience this as well. An uninformed group conscience may build unrealistic expectations about meetings or CoDA groups. Members may control, manipulate, or intimidate other members or violate the Traditions. In these cases, unrealistic expectations and resulting behaviors become self-serving and sabotaging. The good of the whole of CoDA becomes jeopardized. These unhealthy motives or unrealistic expectations can perpetuate codependence within our program. Exploring our motives with our sponsor and CoDA friends prior to engaging in service work is important. Regardless of whether or not we desire or avoid service work, our sponsor can also help us identify the weaker areas of our personal recovery that might be affected.

Before we participate, it helps for us to understand our expectations, weaknesses, and strengths. CoDA offers few specific guidelines for the amount of time a member should remain involved in any service position. We each need to remain aware of our length of service and when it is best to step aside. Others need to rise through the service organization to experience the benefits and growth. Sometimes we hurt ourselves when we remain active in a role or take on more tasks when no one offers to help. When this happens, we run the risk of relapsing into our codependency.

To find out how long we should take on a certain task or role, it's helpful for us to recall our spiritual and personal reasons for engaging in service work. We may journal our thoughts and feelings, pray for insight, and talk with our sponsors and CoDA friends. We need to be sensitive to the appropriate time for us to end our service work in a given area and allow others the opportunity to experience the growth and the spirit of giving that service work offers. For recovering codependents, our service work is a valuable tool. It's not a fix, penance or an arena for control. It's our way of passing on to others what has been given to us.

The Traditions in service work

Our Twelve Traditions are the spiritual principles for the membership of CoDA as a whole and the spiritual guidelines for the provision of service work. They help CoDA to remain spiritually centered and to operate from a state of integrity. They provide us a clear and specific path so that CoDA will continue to be available for us all.

Applying the Traditions and their spiritual principles in service work means learning to speak for ourselves, practicing spiritual equality with others and maintaining boundaries. We learn to accept others' differences, to lovingly confront passive and aggressive abuses, and to work together with others for CoDA's highest good. We learn to be a part of a team working toward, and developing unity within, the CoDA program.

We risk hurting CoDA if we do service work without the guidance of the spiritual principles found in our Traditions. We can prevent this by applying the knowledge and wisdom of the Traditions as well as sharing the experiences of our membership. Understanding and implementing the Traditions is the responsibility of every CoDA member. We find it helpful to study and discuss them with our sponsor and CoDA friends. We also enhance our study by exploring how the Traditions apply to various aspects of service work. Some of the ways individual members or groups can support the healthy functioning of CoDA are through these actions:

- Promoting the use of CoDA Conference endorsed literature at meetings.

- Donating amounts over a group's prudent reserve in the Seventh Tradition.

- Using the group conscience to resolve issues.

- Involving ourselves in service that positively impacts other groups or CoDA as a whole.

- Honoring the anonymity of CoDA members.

Each of us is harmed every time a member or group breaks or modifies any of our Traditions; and each time we ignore, disregard, or overlook Traditions violations, we perpetuate that hurt. The ripple effect can hurt other CoDA groups in the local, regional, national, and/or international com-munities. It is important to speak up when Traditions violations occur. We find it helpful to do so in non-shaming and loving ways. No one is on trial; perhaps the individual or group is not even aware of the Tradition violation. We ask our group to hold a business meeting. We share our knowledge and experience with the Traditions and the issue. We listen as others share their thoughts and opinions. We discuss the issues and look for solutions that best serve CoDA. After all discussions have taken place, we then take a group conscience vote and trust in our Higher Power's will to be expressed through that vote.

Service work is both a gift and a responsibility. As we continuously rely upon the wisdom and guidance of our Twelve Traditions, conditions that can negatively affect CoDA's safety rarely appear. In practicing these principles throughout our service work, we become responsible for safeguarding the spiritual integrity and the future of CoDA. If each of us offers a small contribution of our time and talent to service in CoDA, the needs of CoDA will surely be met, and CoDA will continue to grow. Throughout our service work let us remember: We have but one ultimate authority, a loving Higher Power as expressed to our group conscience, and but one primary purpose—carrying the message to the codependent who still suffers.

CHAPTER FIVE
Commonly Asked Questions

Beginning recovery in CoDA can seem confusing at times. We ask questions and sometimes the answers bring up more questions. CoDA's Fellowship is comprised of a wide variety of people who have gained valuable experience through their lives. This chapter is a collection of our questions and answers over the years. We've found it helpful to refer to these questions and answers throughout our recovery, not only in the early stages, but as a useful reminder as we walk our recovery road.

We're not suggesting that the following paragraphs contain all of the questions about recovery raised by the CoDA Fellowship or that these answers are definitive; however, it's helpful to discuss these topics in meetings or with our sponsor and friends. By doing this, we can hear a wider variety of experience, strength, and hope from our Fellowship, and generate more discussion. As we evolve and grow, our questions and answers will change, too. This chapter, therefore, represents part of the experience, strength, and hope of the Fellowship of CoDA. It is important to remember that the Fellowship of CoDA is not attempting to provide professional or therapeutic help. We're simply offering our understanding of how we've applied these ideas and concepts to our recovery programs.

Why do I need meetings?

The CoDA pamphlet, "Attending Meetings," describes the "building blocks" of recovery: meetings, working the Steps, sponsorship, and service. It also lists how we gain the most benefit from attending CoDA meetings: speaking, sharing and listening.

Meetings are where we hear the experience, strength, and hope of other recovering codependents. We learn to join the camaraderie of people supporting each other in healing. We learn to listen and experience being heard. We find out how others have worked the Twelve Steps and how the Twelve Traditions have influenced their lives.

We learn about ourselves and our relationships with others by hearing other people share about growth and change. We can be present, loving, and supportive of ourselves and each other in healthy and fulfilling ways. As we attend meetings and apply what we learn to our daily lives, we become more loving, caring, accountable, and responsible. Most importantly, meetings remind us from where we've come and how far we've grown. They provide us with a continuous support network throughout our recovery process.

How long do I need to go to CoDA meetings?

Many of us believe we may need to attend CoDA meetings the rest of our lives; others disagree. It's a personal choice and one that requires contemplation. Our decision may vary from year to year as our recovery progresses. No matter how long we're in recovery, we may experience episodes of codependence, although they're not usually as strong or long-lasting as in our early recovery.

Whether or not we choose to attend meetings for the rest of our lives, we believe CoDA always will be there for us.

What is a CoDA birthday?

A CoDA birthday is the annual acknowledgment and personal celebration by each of us of the day we started our codependence recovery within the CoDA program. This birthday can represent our first CoDA meeting or the day we first called ourselves "a codependent." Members at our CoDA meetings often recognize people celebrating birthdays and present them with a medallion for the number of years they've been a part of CoDA. When they do, we recognize that it's a special time for all of us. We can congratulate each other and acknowledge our continued commitment and effort to gain personal recovery and happiness.

What are sponsors?

Sponsors are people within the CoDA program who help guide us through the Twelve Step recovery process. These people are recovering codependents whose personal recovery is their first priority. They continue to learn how to live happy and fulfilling lives and are willing to share their experience, strength and hope with us. They've usually walked the road of recovery longer than we have. They're who we call for help when we're confused or overwhelmed. They can also be friends who work the program with us.

Sponsors are able to remain objective and detached from feeling responsible for our happiness and recovery. They also refrain from behaving in abusive, critical, or controlling ways that can result in fixing, rescuing, acting as therapist, sexual manipulation, or personal gain. Sponsors are role models for recovery, sources of loving support, and respectful of our anonymity and individual pace in working the program.

More information about sponsors can be found in available CoDA literature.

How do I find a sponsor?

The CoDA pamphlet, "Sponsorship In CoDA," lists some suggestions for finding a sponsor when there are few old-timers within our Fellowship:

> New CoDA groups usually have members with long histories in other Twelve Step programs, both as members and as sponsors. While they may not have experience with CoDA's application of the Steps, they do understand what it means to work the Steps in daily life. Such a person may be a candidate to sponsor you. There is a form of sponsorship arising out of this kind of situation called "co-sponsorship." If you choose this method, you and another CoDA member will sponsor each other. You can meet regularly to share what you are learning about the Steps from others and from reading CoDA literature. As you discuss various aspects of the program, you may become aware that each of you has some answers within. Some CoDA members have started sponsorship groups which meet weekly or bi-weekly. This

group consists of people who make a commitment to work on the Twelve Steps together. Discussion is focused on applying the Steps to specific issues that are related to recovery from codependence.

Do I have to believe in God to recover?

Codependence involves a spiritual dilemma, meaning that we've made people our Higher Power, just as alcoholics make alcohol their Higher Power for their sense of well-being. Anything to which we give our power and well-being can become our god. We find this to be true whether we've experienced a belief in a Higher Power or not.

Many of us find that recovering from codependence means believing in a power greater than ourselves, another person, behavior, addiction, place, or thing. Some of us try to recover without this belief but fall short. Through our faith, trust, and belief in a Higher Power, we're able to experience a rich and rewarding recovery from codependence.

As we attend meetings and listen to CoDA members describe their recovery, we hear them talk about a relationship with a Higher Power and notice that those who maintain a regular connection with this power experience the recovery we seek. The form of this Higher Power is ours to discover—whether it be unconditional love, divine intelligence, God, nature, music, an image of an ocean, river or tree, or our own CoDA "home group." Above all, it's important that we become willing to entertain the possibility there is something that can do for us what we cannot do for ourselves.

What is the purpose of prayer and meditation?

Since so much of codependence is tied into our spiritual dilemma, we find that consistently praying and meditating (in whatever form that works for us) improves our conscious contact with our Higher Power and helps keep us on our recovery journey. We can allow fear, projection, blame, and shame to overpower our relationship with our Higher Power if we don't include some type of prayer, meditation, or contact in our daily routine.

Through prayer and meditation, we can experience a sense of peace and serenity in our lives, and strengthen and nurture our relationship with our Higher Power. It's a time we can be ourselves with our Higher Power and affirm that this God of our choosing is there for us. We can focus on our daily purpose, asking that our Higher Power's will be done in our lives and for the power to carry that out.

Why doesn't CoDA refer to God or our Higher Power as He or She?

Many CoDA members have spiritual beliefs that do not interpret God as masculine and/or feminine. Many people in our Fellowship have been discriminated against or suffered physical, sexual, or verbal abuse from the males and females in their lives who were authority figures. Many people have experienced religious abuse in situations where God was referred to in a masculine sense.

As a result, many CoDA members have difficulty separating the messages, shame, fear, and pain from their concept of

God. To them, God has the personality of these abusive and/or neglectful individuals because they held the authority status, so it may be difficult to hear God referred to as "He" or "She."

Given the wide variety of people, cultures, and countries, CoDA chooses to extend respect to all people and their varied spiritual beliefs. In short, CoDA simply refers to God as our Higher Power.

Do I work the Steps only one time?

Throughout the recovery process, we work the Steps many times. They're not meant to be a one time fix. Our Twelfth Step tells us to practice these principles in all of our affairs, which is our guidance to work the Steps every time we discover an area of our lives over which we're powerless. Each time we give someone the power to affect our well-being, the Steps help us to regain our empowerment and learn from the situation.

The Steps are our guides to living and maintaining healthy lives. By following this guidance we are given tools to use for a lifetime.

What is "Thirteenth-Stepping?"

This term originated in several other Twelve Step programs to describe unhealthy and inappropriate sexual behaviors that take place within the Fellowship. One person could be taking advantage of another when he or she is in a vulnerable or painful spot, or someone may be using a nurturing hug for sexual gratification. It could apply to sexual innuendoes or sexual joking in order to control, embarrass, or subtly negotiate sexually with another. Thirteenth-Stepping also occurs in meetings when members flirt, dress inappropriately, or attend just to find dates.

In an attempt to approach the subject without shame and blame (because many people are unaware of these behaviors), some members of the Fellowship make announcements or engage in discussions concerning Thirteenth-Stepping and the potential damage it can cause. Whether we're engaging in inappropriate behaviors, receiving, or witnessing them, we must all work together to create and maintain CoDA meetings where the members can feel safe to be vulnerable, share their thoughts and feelings, and receive support for their recovery without manipulation or control.

What does childhood have to do with our lives today?

The habits and beliefs of a lifetime, from how often we brush our teeth to ideas about God, country, and our place in the world, are established in childhood. As we continue our recovery work in CoDA, we find many of the thoughts, feelings, and behaviors of childhood are present in our adult lives. Until we consciously examine each, we may unconsciously continue these habits and adhere to the beliefs we learned as children. The CoDA *Welcome* states, *"...that codependence is a most deeply-rooted, compulsive behavior, and that it is born out of our sometimes moderately, sometimes extremely dysfunctional family systems."* The roots referred to in the phrase, *"...deeply-rooted, compulsive behaviors"* can often be uncovered and traced to the experiences of childhood. More importantly, the way we interpreted these experiences and the coping devices we created to overcome our distress allowed us to survive or even thrive. We continued to use and perfect these methods of coping until they became unconscious parts of ourselves.

In our current relationships with others, we tend to repeat our dysfunctional patterns of the past. As adults, especially when our lives become difficult, we often revert to the old familiar behaviors to deal with current feelings and situations rather than question our long held beliefs. For example, if, as children, we experienced a raging parent, as adults, we may experience fear of anger—our own or others. Rather than express ourselves directly or honestly, we may go to great lengths to avoid confrontation. Conversely, if we identify with the aggressor, we may become argumentative and controlling. Codependence is about extremes.

If, as children, we were emotionally or physically neglected, we may find ourselves attracted to people who are consistently preoccupied, absent, or emotionally unavailable. Or, we may perpetuate the abuse cycle through our own actions or inactions. If, as children, we were physically abused, as adults we may become attracted to insecure, aggressive partners because their behaviors are familiar—reminding us of one or more of our caregivers. Or, we may justify and imitate their behavior, using physical force in our attempts to control others.

If, as children, we were emotionally abused, we may verbally abuse our partners or we may choose partners who emotionally abuse us. If, as children, we were sexually abused, we may have learned to use our sexuality in a manipulative way to get what we wanted, or we may be indiscriminate in our sexual relations because we confuse sex with love. We may not feel able to refuse sex, or we may avoid sexual situations entirely. If, as children, we were expected to be perfect, we may continue this illusion and rarely, if ever, feel satisfied with our own or others' performances, looks, and/or accomplishments.

We answer the Step One questions in Chapter Three to begin understanding how our powerlessness developed in childhood. Working the First Step helps us to gain an awareness of the effect our behaviors have had on our lives. ("We admitted we were powerless over others—that our lives had become unmanageable.") As adults continually focusing on our recovery, we work the Fourth Step, which helps us to further identify and admit to these behaviors. As we take a long, hard look at ourselves, deeply buried feelings begin to surface, bringing about the awareness that, at times, we have acted as a victim or victimizer due to our childhood experiences.

Searching for clarity and becoming more aware of the adverse effects of our childhood behavioral patterns, we seek help. We use the tools of the program; i.e., we call our sponsor, attend and share at meetings, keep a journal, and seek out supportive CoDA members or friends. Most importantly, we rely on our Higher Power for guidance. Our recovery work helps us move forward in our healing process and release the powerful hold of the past.

What is the child-within?

The child-within is the sum of all of our childhood experiences, memories, perceptions, beliefs, and emotions. It is the part of us that 1) experienced both the positive and the negative aspects of childhood; 2) retains the unexpressed feelings generated by our childhood experiences; and 3) reacts strongly, either passively or rebelliously, to the difficult situations we encounter in our adult lives.

The child-within, or our inner-child, is that part of us that carries the innocence of life, curiosity of nature, and the spirit of who we are. Our inner-child can be delightful, spontaneous, creative, playful, joyful, mischievous, tender, and loving. It may also appear as the hurt, embittered, shamed, scared, or angry part of us.

When unsettling feelings connected with the past are triggered, the child-within often reacts impulsively, immaturely, or aggressively. Our unresolved issues erupt as overwhelming thoughts and/or feelings that drive our behaviors, often leaving us wondering, "Why did I act like that?" or "Where did *that* come from?"

For example, if criticized by someone, we may overreact in anger, or we may be passive. We might go into a shame spiral without realizing that we are actually reacting to a similar event from childhood, when we were shamed or criticized. A minor loss may bring on bouts of uncontrollable crying and subsequent depression, which actually relates back to unexpressed grief from childhood. For instance, as a child, we may have experienced the death of a loved one, but were told not to cry.

The solution lies, not with trying to eradicate the child-within, but by embracing this often unpredictable, sometimes unwelcome part of ourselves. With help from our Higher Power, as we experience and accept our inner-child, we are able to heal our pain from the past and discover our authentic selves. Learning to accept and love ourselves is a gift we give ourselves, allowing us to live healthier, happier lives. We are able to experience what it means to love and to be loved. Recovery work is vital if we want to free ourselves from our all-consuming fears and resentments of the past. Attending meetings, following others' examples, learning to have fun, journal writing, and seeking professional assistance, if necessary, are some of the ways we use to connect with the precious little child within.

What is meant by parenting ourselves?

Parenting or reparenting ourselves means recognizing we are capable human beings who are choosing to become fully-functioning, emotionally healthy adults. Growing up in dysfunctional families left us with many unmet needs, and we may not have felt valued or loved by our parents. As adults in recovery we become aware of our childhood wounds, and we have the opportunity to fill those childhood voids. We learn to take care of ourselves by honoring and setting limits with our inner child. We use our recovery tools to nurture ourselves, develop healthy boundaries, and become accountable for our actions. As we come to love ourselves, we are capable of loving others and accepting love in return. We place our faith in a Higher Power and ask for help in addressing the fears, hurts, shame, and anger of the child-within.

Parenting ourselves means reflecting on and responding to situations, rather than reacting. It means practicing acceptance and asking for what we want and need in relationships. We strive to let go of self-shame and blame and take responsibility for ourselves, our happiness, and our sorrow. As we become more able to take care of ourselves, we discover how to stop expecting others to fulfill our basic needs.

Healthy parenting self-talk is filled with honesty, strength, understanding, compassion, and wisdom. If we make a mistake, our parent-self or inner parent refrains from making self-shaming statements. Instead, we address the mistake with a compassionate inner dialogue such as, "I know I made a mistake; I feel sad and guilty about it, but I'm human—sometimes I make mistakes." We nurture ourselves with loving behaviors and thoughts.

Learning to parent ourselves is a continuous process requiring a variety of teachers. Observing and listening to healthy mothers and fathers talk to their children provides models of good parenting skills. For those of us who were shamed by our parents, we discover we can reparent our inner child with a nurturing inner parent we choose to create for ourselves. We let go of negative shame-based beliefs and reparent ourselves with affirmations and permissions that help us recover from childhood wounds. Recovery allows us to be our authentic selves.

We can read books that cover parenting, assertiveness training, affirmations, and building self-esteem. Sponsors and CoDA friends may share with us their own self-parenting journey. Such examples can help us learn about loving behaviors and dialogue between our inner parent and inner child. Along with the wisdom, love, and accountability found in our Twelve Steps and Twelve Traditions, a loving Higher Power is our greatest teacher.

What are boundaries?

A boundary is a limit or border. In CoDA, boundaries relate to imaginary borders that surround each individual's body, spirit, energy, behaviors, thoughts, and emotions. We set boundaries to help insure our personal safety, comfort, and self-respect. If our boundaries are violated by ourselves or others, we experience various feelings of discomfort. Thus, we use our boundaries to care for ourselves and to be respectful of others.

We distinguish between external and internal boundaries. External boundaries focus on physical and sexual aspects. Internal boundaries concentrate on protecting our emotional, mental, and spiritual well-being. If our boundaries are intact and functional, then we can say: "I know where I stop and where you begin," "I know what is my business and what is none of my business," "I know the difference between my emotions and others' emotions," "I recognize what is and is not my responsibility," and "I am aware of what is and is not comfortable or safe for me."

An example of a physical (external) boundary is a personal comfort zone: the distance of space that feels comfortable between two people. If we do not know a person, we might not feel safe if the person gets too close, tries to hug us, or physically touches us. When we close or lock a door for privacy, or tell someone we do not want a hug, we are setting a physical boundary so we can feel safe. Our physical boundary (comfort zone) can also be flexible. It can vary for different relationships and it can change within a relationship because of circumstances. We are all unique and only we can determine what physical boundaries feel safe and appropriate for us.

We are also responsible for and have the right to determine our sexual boundaries. As stated in the *Newcomers Handbook*, "Healthy and safe sexual boundaries are recommended from the very beginning in CoDA. It is not wise to begin new sexual or love relationships when first attending CoDA. Anesthetizing the pain of failed codependent relationships by immediately beginning a new relationship is a part of the disease. Staying out of new sexual relationships is a good stop-gap to end the dysfunctional behavior long enough to figure out what is going on inside."

Some of us may have experienced sexual abuse at some time during our lives and may not recognize healthy sexual boundaries. In recovery, we take our time getting to know our true selves and determining what is safe and comfortable for ourselves. We also take time to know a potential partner before deciding if it is appropriate to be sexual with that person. Even if we have previously been sexual with someone, we have the prerogative to say "no" to additional sexual encounters. No one has the right to be sexual with us without our permission. We do not have to engage in any type of sexual activity that feels unsafe, inappropriate, or uncomfortable. We always have the right to say "no" or tell someone to stop at any time before or during sexual activity.

Our internal boundaries define and contain the unique personal characteristics of our thoughts, feelings, opinions, behaviors, beliefs, and spirituality. Boundaries help us recognize, honor, and respect our individual wants, needs, and desires. They help us define our separateness and give us safety in our intimate communications with others. If someone verbally attacks us, we maintain our internal boundary and practice self-containment by moderately expressing our thoughts and feelings about their behavior using "I" statements. Or, we may choose not to respond and silently remind ourselves that how another person acts is about that person, not about us. If someone confronts us about our behavior, we use our internal boundary to listen to what they say. We do not internalize what is said before deciding if any of it rings true for us. If we have wronged the other person, we make amends. In either situation our self-worth is not diminished because we have maintained our internal boundaries.

We use internal boundaries in various ways. An example is deciding how much personal information, such as personal history or financial information, to share with others. Conversely, we refrain from delving into others' personal business. We might really want to ask a question or say something to someone, yet we do not because we know that person's private life is none of our business.

When we have healthy internal boundary systems, we recognize that each individual is responsible for his or her emotional, mental, and spiritual boundaries. We allow ourselves and others to have their own thoughts, feelings, opinions, behaviors, beliefs, and spirituality. With functional boundaries we are able to meet our needs without infringing on others' abilities to meet their needs. Our internal boundaries can be flexible, and we decide what is safe and comfortable for ourselves.

We are the only ones who can engage our own boundaries. We cannot expect others to recognize and respect them if they do not know about them. It is our responsibility to communicate our boundaries to others in a gentle and firm way, remembering that if someone hasn't dealt with their own lack of boundaries, they probably will not recognize boundaries in others. If we encounter a perpetrator or major offender who does not respect our boundaries, then it might be necessary to create a "wall" between us and that person for our personal safety. Conversely, some of us may avoid forming healthy and loving relationships by shutting ourselves off from authentic interactions with others. We may believe we have created boundaries when we have actually created walls that impede our ability to have healthy relationships.

Creating healthy boundaries is essential for our recovery. We learn this by attending meetings, socializing after meetings, talking with our sponsor, working the Steps, and participating in service work. With the guidance we receive from our Higher Power, we create healthy boundaries for ourselves and learn to respect others' boundaries. We are then able to form and sustain healthy and loving relationships with ourselves and others.

What is enmeshment?

Enmeshment occurs in relationships between people who have not developed their own clear identities and/or boundaries. Each person's sense of wholeness and self-worth is intertwined with those of the other person. It is as if there were only one identity, and it is difficult for either to function fully without the other. When we look to another person to define our values, and we accept their needs, feelings, or opinions as our own, we are enmeshed. Statements of enmeshment such as, "I'd die without you," "You're my everything," "Without you, I'm nothing," "I need you," or "You make me whole," are found in everyday conversations.

Enmeshment is common among family members, lovers, friends, and in caretaking situations. An enmeshed relationship doesn't allow for individuality, autonomy, wholeness, or personal empowerment. Healthy relationships with ourselves, others, and with our Higher Power are hindered by enmeshment because our focus is most often outward, towards someone else.

The antidote for enmeshment is developing healthy boundaries, keeping the focus on ourselves, and working to define our unique identities, wants, needs, and opinions. Maintaining a relationship with our Higher Power, participating in CoDA meetings, and using the Twelve Steps and Twelve Traditions in our relationships with others all help us let go of our enmeshment behaviors and become our authentic selves.

What is detachment?

Detachment is the act of disengaging or disconnecting from another person, group of people, or situation. Detaching allows us to emotionally and/or physically separate ourselves from people, events, and places in order to gain a healthy, objective point of view. If we don't like the behavior of others, we can detach, recognizing that we are separate from them with our own distinct identity and set of boundaries. We endeavor to detach with love and respect for ourselves and others, especially when detaching from family or friends. We ask our Higher Power to help us focus on maintaining our boundaries. Even though we care, we remember that we are not responsible for other people's behaviors, nor are they responsible for our well-being.

What is the difference between detachment and avoidance?

Another way of stating this could be, "What is the difference between letting go and running away?"

In CoDA, detachment is a conscious act of self-care. We choose to disengage emotionally from people and/or leave situations that could harm us. Avoidance is often an unconscious, dysfunctional coping mechanism that allows us to avoid self-accountability, ignore people or situations, hide from the truth, or run away from our responsibilities. Avoidance is often driven by our fear of experiencing rejection, anger, disappointment, abandonment, or shame. Simply put, detachment is an action based on love and strength while avoidance is based on fear.

Am I ever recovered from codependence?

We can become very disappointed if we believe we can stop all of our codependent behaviors. Our program reminds us to show up, work our recovery process and turn the results over to God. When we do this and release perfectionism, we can experience the hope and miracles of recovery: a life progressively filled with serenity, acceptance, and love.

What is a codependent slip?

Dictionaries tell us that the word slip means to stumble, fall, make an error or mistake. When we apply that to our codependence, we find the same meaning; we momentarily return to using codependent behaviors to deal with interactions or life's circumstances. (A codependent slip is also called backsliding.)

We remember there's not complete abstinence in our recovery; we're human and make mistakes. How we deal with those mistakes is what's more important. Our Tenth Step helps us to address this: "Continued to take personal inventory and when we were wrong, promptly admitted it." We also try to remember that our mistakes help us to determine what aspects of our recovery we should work on, and we ask our Higher Power for help.

If we continue to slip, we may consider reworking the Steps on that issue. This will enable us to reach a deeper level of healing and understanding about the problem and work toward healthier behaviors.

We've also found it helpful to avoid shaming or punishing ourselves for our slips. Remembering that shame is a large part of codependence, we find we only fuel the fire when we add self-shaming and punishment to our mistakes. Forgiveness, love, and perseverance from our self-parent are the keys to working with our codependent slips.

What is meant by bottom-line behaviors?

A "bottom-line behavior" is a situation or a specific behavior that is likely to trigger our codependence. In order to maintain emotional sobriety and advance recovery we avoid these situations and behaviors. For example, an alcoholic avoids taking that first drink; a gambler avoids casinos, lottery tickets, etc.; and a compulsive eater avoids foods or behavior that can cause an eating binge.

For codependents, our bottom-line behaviors can manifest in different, complex forms depending on how we act out in our disease. We look at behaviors that have been offensive or hurtful to ourselves and others. These may include remaining in relationships with toxic people, accepting sex as a substitute for love, trying to rescue others, pleasing others at our own expense, obsessive thinking, fantasizing, attempting to control people or circumstances, and condemning ourselves.

We ask our Higher Power for guidance, talk with our sponsor, read inspirational literature and review our Fourth Step for renewed awareness of these behaviors. Each one of us determines what our individual bottom-line behaviors are. We seek out and create guidelines for ourselves—recovery tools to help us abstain from acting-out these behaviors. If we have a codependent slip and engage in one of our bottom-line behaviors, we practice self-love by forgiving ourselves. Our fear and shame subside as we become more accountable for our behaviors and actively work on changing them.

What is a shame spiral?

When we experience overwhelming feelings of worthlessness, apathy, or panic, we may believe there is no solution or end to our pain. Our feelings/beliefs seem to take on a life of their own and we feel isolated, rejected, foolish, or stupid. We may berate or push ourselves harder to meet someone else's expectations, engage in unhealthy sexual behavior, compulsively eat or starve ourselves, or try to escape from a situation by avoiding people. All of these behaviors cause our negative feelings to intensify and we feel more pain and confusion. We call this a shame spiral. Without intervention, our shame will spiral even more and may result in a crisis situation.

To counteract the shame spiral, it is important to reach out for guidance and support—to our Higher Power, to our sponsor, and to our non-judgmental recovery friends. Writing about our thoughts and feelings, talking with people we trust, attending meetings, and nurturing our inner child with affirmations can help decrease the intensity of our shame. With recovery, we choose to focus on our strengths and possible solutions in order to regain a sense of empowerment and self-esteem.

What is fear of shame?

Fear of shame is our fear of being shamed again by our boss, mate, family members, friends or parents. It has much greater control of our lives than shame itself.

We may be afraid to hear about our mistakes or shortcomings and, in turn, become defensive or critical, possibly avoiding or lying about a situation. We become terrified of being discounted or abandoned. We control others out of fear of their disappointment or anger with us. The shame we fear most is the same type of shame we experienced in our childhood.

Many of us find it helpful to share these fears with our sponsor or friends. When we confront these feelings and the resulting progressive fears, we're able to soothe and possibly eliminate their intensity.

What is projection?

Projection is a type of denial we use to cope with our unrecognized characteristics and/or unresolved issues, both present and past. It is as if we are a movie projector and a present life situation and/or another person functions as the screen. We may project a painful memory or a disowned characteristic onto this "screen" and convince ourselves that what we are "seeing or experiencing" is reality.

One form of projection is when we react from our history by re-creating an unhealthy childhood relationship or situation. We take an unresolved feeling/issue from our past and believe it is happening now in our current relationship. In essence, we are unknowingly projecting our past onto the present moment.

Another form of projection occurs when we displace an unresolved past or unwanted present feeling, such as anger, onto others. In projecting one of our disowned behaviors or feelings onto others, we might accuse them of being angry, or we might convince ourselves that they are angry with us. For example, we may lie to a friend. In order to avoid experiencing the feelings (regret, anxiety, guilt, shame) that might accompany our admission of lying, we instead accuse the friend of lying to us. We remain in denial by accusing others of behavior that is our own to correct.

What are physical and aggressive forms of abuse and control?

Some people say that identifying physical and aggressive forms of abuse and control is a simple task. We've found there are many forms of abuse and control that are difficult to recognize. Outlined below are three areas of obvious and subtle forms of physical and aggressive abuse and control.

> **Physical pain:** Any physical behavior that results in creating physical pain in ourselves or another, including pinching, scratching, biting, slapping, hitting, kicking, or repeated injuries due to physical activities such as overexertion, forcing the body to attempt to reach unrealistic expectations, unnecessary surgeries and/or medical treatment that would result in physical pain.

Physical restraints: These include obsessive tickling, ganging up on another, holding someone down against his/her will, hair pulling and restraining any physical movement or physical freedom against someone's will.

Sexual touch: Fondling, being forced or coerced into sexually touching or kissing another person, sexual hugging, unwanted kissing or touch, molestation, rape and sexual violence, or any sexual behavior used to control another.

What are non-physical and passive forms of abuse and control?

We've found eight areas which help identify some of the nonphysical forms of abuse and control.

Criticism: Shaming, put-downs, mocking, blaming, name-calling, imitating or taunting others, insinuations, and using meaningless words or gestures.

Verbal abuse: Shouting, being vulgar, continuously raging, using profanity, angry expressions or gestures to control.

Misrepresenting: Falsifying, exaggerating, distorting, lying, withholding and/or misstating information and being unfaithful.

Dominating: Domineering, controlling, claiming to know the truth, commanding, or analyzing others' behavior through logic or shame.

Suppressing others emotionally: Refusing to offer support, attention, respect or validation of others' feelings; not offering affirmations or compliments.

Denying self-care: Needlessness, or not asking for help and support; addictions to alcohol, drugs, food, sex, or other substances; people-pleasing, caretaking, or isolation.

Financial constraints: Controlling the spending of others; non-support of a partner's desire to work; withholding money; using money or resources as punishment; making financial promises with no intention of keeping them.

Power tactics: Hurrying others to make decisions; shaming, accusing, pouting, threatening, or manipulating others; abusing feelings; gathering forces to control others; using money, sex, children, or religion to control.

What's the difference between being codependent and being thoughtful?

Very simply, our motivation tells us the difference. If our motivation for being thoughtful is fear-based and of any need to fix, caretake, control, manipulate, or avoid abandonment, we're behaving codependently. If our motivation is a sincere desire to give to another person with no fear of shame, abandonment or neglect of our needs and boundaries, then we're being thoughtful.

When we find ourselves pleasing other people and behaving in ways that can be harmful to our needs, we should ask ourselves, "Have I taken care of myself?" This question can help us discern our motivation to care for others.

What's the difference between blame and accountability?

We blame others when we're using victim-like behaviors, when we refuse to take responsibility for our lives, safety, well-being, and happiness. We may believe the unhappiness in our lives is caused by our mates, parents, jobs or even God, but our unhappiness is actually caused by our own feelings and thoughts. As long as we blame other people, we're powerless to do anything constructive toward recovery. We're like a mouse caught in a maze of our own creation. Accountability is taking responsibility for our feelings, thoughts, behaviors, and solutions. We stop longing for others to make us happy and look to ourselves and our God.

How do I learn to trust?

Many of us are never taught when or how to trust. The words we heard from our childhood may have been, "I love you," but the behaviors we saw weren't loving. So as children, we learned early not to trust. Today, we may isolate from interactions, or become overly trusting, setting ourselves up for hurt and disappointment. Learning to trust others appropriately doesn't happen until we're able to trust ourselves and our Higher Power. These relationships need to be in order first, so that we're better able to understand the trustworthy behaviors of others. This enables us to develop trust within our relationships.

Do I have to forgive those who hurt me?

There's a saying within CoDA: "Blame keeps wounds open, and forgiveness lets wounds heal." If we want to heal, we must learn to forgive. Not forgiving at all keeps us bound to blaming. It serves only to perpetuate our resentments and hurts. Quickly seeking and/or forgiving early in our recovery often becomes a quick fix. We must first do Steps One through Seven before approaching Step Eight. If not, personal and emotional growth do not take place. Forgiveness or not, our same codependent patterns eventually repeat themselves.

How do I apply my recovery to my relationships?

All healthy relationships require our consistent time, patience, attention and nurturing. Many of our relationships have been devastated by our codependence. How do we begin the process of healing? How do we move from being fearful human beings to becoming loving, healthy and empowered individuals who allow others to be the same? The Steps give us the guidance and direction we need.

We may find it helpful to look at our relationships in their order of importance to us, focusing first on our relationship with ourselves, our Higher Power, our mate; then children, family, friends, and finally those at work. We work the Twelve Steps with our sponsor about each relationship—past and present. We may discover that their order of importance changes as we become healthier human beings. We look at our powerlessness within and about each relationship, and focus on what we've experienced with them. We look to see where we've projected our childhood experiences into our adult relationships and how we've recreated these patterns again. We ask our Higher Power for help and insight.

Many of us take time to imagine what our behaviors might be like if our relationships were loving, healthy, and equal. We note what positive changes we've done, so that we can focus on new positive changes each day.

Our Step work may include issues of powerlessness and unmanageability about the relationship. We explore our definitions of what we've been taught about relationships. We look at our roles within them, as well as our expectations of the other person's roles.

We talk with our sponsor about learning new ways to communicate with others. We take responsibility for our feelings, needs, and wants and share them within our relationship. We search for meetings where topics focusing on relationships can help us learn how to improve our behaviors in these areas. Some of us feel additional need to seek professional help for overwhelming issues beyond the guidance and support that CoDA can offer.

When both individuals (or a family) are willing to recover—both individually and together—then healthy, loving, caring, and truly intimate relationships can emerge. Developing and maintaining healthy and loving relationships is a lifelong process. It helps us as individuals to develop mutual support and respect for the relationship and one another's growth. We understand how we all grow and evolve, and that we deserve each other's patience and care. Recovery and the Steps offer us the tools to maintain this process.

Can I use CoDA for all my addictions?

Though codependence is considered the root of all addictions, CoDA doesn't address specific information or aid in the recovery from other addictions and compulsive behaviors. Members of our Fellowship who identify other compulsive and/

or addictive behaviors should also attend the appropriate Twelve Step program that can help them address their issues. Results can be disastrous when CoDA members attempt to circumvent their need for other Twelve Step programs by using CoDA as their sole recovery program.

As we begin our recovery from codependence, some of our discoveries and experiences can become emotionally overwhelming. When this happens, those of us who have other addictive and compulsive behaviors, and who are not doing Twelve Step recovery work for these behaviors, can find that our addictions intensify. This may lead us to get involved (or re-involved) in Twelve Step programs that are applicable for our unique recovery.

Some of us relapse with other addictions before we're willing to get involved with another program. Regrettably, some members of the CoDA Fellowship have died as a result.

It is strongly suggested that we not use CoDA as the sole recovery program for all our addictions and compulsive behaviors.

What is the difference between CoDA, Al-Anon, Adult Children of Alcoholics (ACA/ACoA) and Al-Anon Adult Children (AAAC)?

Al-Anon, Adult Children of Alcoholics and Al-Anon Adult Children are Fellowships for those who are spouses, family members, or friends of alcoholics. CoDA is a Fellowship for those who have difficulty in maintaining healthy, functional relationships with others, regardless of whether those others have alcohol, drug, or other problems. Members of CoDA may also be members of these other Twelve Step Fellowships.

Do I need professional help because I'm codependent?

Many members of CoDA's Fellowship seek the help of the professional community. It's an individual choice, not a requirement. CoDA is a nonprofessional organization and cannot assess a member's need for professional guidance, counseling, or therapy. Many of us seek professional help for issues related to our codependence that are beyond the scope of the experience, strength, and hope that the CoDA program and our Fellowship offer.

When considering this choice, we find it helpful to ask our Higher Power for guidance and to talk with our sponsor and recovery friends for their experience and support.

Can you recommend any books about codependence? ...or a therapist, hospital or treatment center?

We recommend that members of the Fellowship read CoDA Conference endorsed publications and listen to the stories of CoDA members in recovery. These publications and audio recordings are available from CoRe Publications. Other books, of course, are read and used by CoDA members, but CoDA, as a Fellowship, cannot recommend or endorse specific books outside approved CoDA literature. We honor Tradition Six by not endorsing any other literature, program, individual, or institution.

CoDA's First Six Years

Ken and Mary R., founders of Co-Dependents Anonymous (CoDA), believe they were spiritually guided in translating the principles of Alcoholics Anonymous (AA) into a life-sustaining program of recovery for codependence.

Ken and Mary believe that seeds of inspiration were planted within them as they experienced a movie depicting the life of Mohandas Gandhi. Both were moved by Gandhi's courageous efforts to help the people of India gain their freedom and independence. Witnessing how one person's work could have such far-reaching effects, they began to think about their own lives and how they might make a difference.

Both Ken and Mary had been in recovery from alcoholism and drug abuse for many years and were well aware of the Twelve Step way of life. They prayed together, in earnest, for God to show them the way.

Mary:

"Passing on the gifts of recovery was so important to us. We were willing to make ourselves available to our Higher Power, to use us in whatever way He chose, so that we might somehow make a difference in this lifetime."

After praying, as they had learned through their Twelve Step recovery experience, they "let go and let God."

During the next three or four years, Ken and Mary experienced both hardships and triumphs. Although they didn't realize it at the time, a Higher Power was at work in their lives, preparing them for what was to come. Ken was working as the Director of Treatment in a residential facility that treated codependence and other addictive behaviors. Both Ken and Mary had begun therapy to deal with their own codependence issues. Over time, they had felt an ever increasing need for fellowship with other codependents.

Ken:

"I found that many of the patients in treatment for codependence were facing the same dilemma that Mary and I were facing. Once they returned home, these patients found little or no fellowship or support to help them in working the Twelve Steps for codependence issues.

It was becoming clear that it was time for me to explore the idea of starting a support group for codependents."

Ken and Mary saw the value in maintaining the spiritual principles found in the Twelve Steps and Twelve Traditions of Alcoholics Anonymous.

Mary:

"We wanted a group specifically focused on the issues of codependence and recovery from codependence, but it had to be based on the Twelve Steps, Twelve Traditions, and principles found in Alcoholics Anonymous. We wanted a group where we could work on our codependence issues both individually and as a couple." During the summer of 1986, Ken and Mary discussed their ideas for a group at length. Then, seeking support, they presented their ideas to friends in recovery. Ken was pleasantly surprised that people were open to the idea.

"It was an exciting time. Everyone was enthusiastic. We held an organizational meeting at our home, inviting anyone who had expressed an interest. Mary M., Renee P., and Craig B. attended. Together we determined the information, materials and steps we'd have to take to hold the first meeting. We adopted the name Co-Dependents Anonymous."

Since AA had over 50 years of success with alcoholism recovery using the Twelve Steps and Twelve Traditions, the group agreed to adopt AA's Steps and Traditions as the heart of the CoDA program. Ken contacted Alcoholics Anonymous for written permission to adapt the Twelve Steps and Twelve Traditions. Permission was granted as long as CoDA was willing to print AA's original Steps and Traditions along with those of CoDA. Mary M. agreed to compile a list of codependent characteristics. The list would help people attending the meeting to identify their issues of codependence. Ken agreed to write the Preamble, the Welcome, the meeting format, and to adapt the Steps and Traditions for CoDA's needs.

The next step was to find a meeting place. Mary recalls how difficult a task that was.

"Weeks went by. We called churches and schools, but could not find any that would be willing to house CoDA's first meeting. The problems we faced were 'not enough space,' 'high liability insurance rates,' 'no time available on the schedule' and extremely high rents. Finally, I spoke with a priest at a church in Phoenix. He graciously agreed to rent CoDA a meeting space. Later, we discovered that one of the initial members of the Board of Trustees belonged to that church." During this time, Craig B., Renee P., and Mary R. had been accumulating supplies and spreading the word about the meeting. Wendy Lee B. designed the trademark and flyer, and Jenise A. created the CoDA Teddy Bear which became the first CoDA logo. And so it began. The first meeting of Co-Dependents Anonymous was held on October 22, 1986, and drew approximately 30 people. Some people came out of curiosity. Some were friends and came to support Ken and Mary. Others came because they had tried different programs and had not found the type of support they needed.

Ken R. chaired the meeting and shared his story. Afterward the meeting broke into small groups for sharing.

Ken:

"It was the first time that any of us were able to openly and freely hear the experience, strength and hope of recovery from codependence. Through the depth and vulnerability of the sharing that took place, it was apparent to many of us that Co-Dependents Anonymous was a program truly inspired by a loving Higher

Power. God had indeed answered the prayers we had uttered four years before."

The following Wednesday, Mary R. shared her story. Attendance at the second CoDA meeting had doubled in size. Within four weeks, the meeting had grown to over 100 people. During the first month, CoDA had to change meeting rooms three times to accommodate the growing number of members.

As the weeks went on, excitement and enthusiasm for the support that CoDA offered continued to build. More CoDA meetings began forming in the Phoenix area. Within the first six months of CoDA's existence, two informational magazine articles were written about the program. These articles, along with meeting starter packets, were distributed by a local treatment center to patients returning to their homes all over the country. Through these and similar efforts, meeting representatives began registering their groups throughout the United States, as well as Sweden. Many people had already pioneered independent codependence support groups throughout the country. They adapted their groups to CoDA's structure and registered them as CoDA groups. Ken and Mary soon realized that CoDA needed a development plan and a structure to aid its rapid development. Again, they turned to their Higher Power for help.

Ken:

"Our prayers were answered through Jim S. He had a solid background in Twelve Step program structure, both on the local and national level, and a working knowledge of the law. Jim was a valuable addition to our group. He graciously offered us his time, direction, experience and services."

They decided to adopt an organizational structure similar to that of Alcoholics Anonymous. AA had survived and grown for more than 50 years with the understanding that each member would have a voice in the decisions and direction of the program.

Mary:

"We recognized that as CoDA's individual members continued to grow and evolve, so would its organization and structure. We decided to adapt AA's Conference Plan and Service Structure to CoDA's needs as a starting point. We wanted the membership of CoDA as a whole to continue to explore and expand. We felt this could be accomplished through the wisdom and guidance of a loving Higher Power, the Twelve Traditions, and a group conscience vote at the annual CoDA Service Conference."

Jim guided Ken and Mary through the process of adapting the AA structure for CoDA's purpose. He also helped them to incorporate a National Board of Trustees and, later, a National Service Office. Jim, with the help of Lane S., wrote the Articles of Incorporation and Bylaws for which CoDA was established. CoDA was incorporated on February 10, 1987.

Jim suggested they appoint seven members with diverse skills and occupations to form the initial CoDA Board of Trustees. The first meeting of the Board was held on February 25, 1987. In attendance were Bill T., Donna P., John M., Donna L., Bill S., Jim S., John J., and Ken and Mary. Ken was elected as Chairperson; John M. became Vice-Chairperson. Mary was elected as Treasurer, and Donna P. became Secretary.

Committees were established to effectively balance the work load of addressing CoDA's growing needs. Each Trustee was charged with the responsibility of recruiting CoDA volunteers to support the committees which included a Finance Committee, the Bear Facts Committee (the original national CoDA newsletter which is now called Co-NNections), a Hospital and Institution Committee, a Literature Committee, an Executive Committee and the National Service Office (N.S.O.).

The Board accepted the challenge to implement a National Service Structure and Conference Plan so that each member of CoDA would have an opportunity to take part in its business and growth. Through the dedication, long hours spent, and love of the first Board of Trustees, CoDA was able to reach and support many individuals in need of recovery from codependence. The National Service Office operated out of Ken and Mary's home for the first seven months.

Mary:

"Our home phone number became CoDA's first national number, and a Glendale, Arizona, post office box became CoDA's first national mailing address. We received hundreds of phone calls and letters from people wanting information about the disease of codependence and about the Co-Dependents Anonymous program. We spent many nights reading letters, corresponding with the CoDA Fellowship, and returning phone calls. We often shared tears of joy reading the many letters people wrote describing the help they received at their local CoDA meetings."

Ken:

"Times were often overwhelming; we answered phone calls for help at 3 a.m.; attempted to operate on not enough sleep; and tried to balance family, recovery, careers and marriage. In addition to answering N.S.O. correspondence, we mailed meeting starter packets, processed registrations and finances and still tried to find time for ourselves! What carried us through was the love and strength of our Higher Power, and the loving support of recovery friends such as Barbara and Curly M., Bill S., John M., Donna L., and many other people too numerous to mention." As the number of calls and letters grew, it became clear that a formal National Service Office needed to be established. Again, Ken and Mary's prayers for help were answered—this time through a CoDA recovering family. Jack M., Betty Lou M., John M. and Nancy M. graciously donated office space, equipment and furniture for the National Service Office. The computer equipment is still in use today.

Nancy M. volunteered to manage the N.S.O. and later accepted the volunteer title of Administrator. She devoted much of her time and skills developing a volunteer force that could meet the fast-growing needs of CoDA. The many hours she spent organizing and managing the National Service Office paid off. Within six months, CoDA had received enough donations to begin paying its own rent! The Board saw this as the achievement of a primary goal, whereby CoDA could maintain autonomy and adhere to the Traditions.

When CoDA was approximately seven months old, the Board of Trustees began the work of planning CoDA's first

National Conference. Elected CoDA representatives from cities nationwide, and Sweden, were invited to participate. On October 2, 1987, just three weeks short of CoDA's first birthday, the first CoDA National Service Conference was held in Phoenix, Arizona.

Mary:

"We were very pleased with the attendance. There were 29 representatives from seven states, the Board of Trustees and the N.S.O. employees. Many people described the experience as a cooperative, intensely spiritual business meeting. There was a profound sense of love, caring and unity. Some people referred to it as the spiritual birthing of CoDA on a national level." At the Conference, Ken and Mary and the Board of Trustees relinquished the future direction of CoDA to the membership and to the guidance of a loving Higher Power as expressed through the group conscience vote. The previous year's work by Ken and Mary, the Board of Trustees and their committees was reviewed by the Conference. Plans for the following year were outlined and set in motion by Conference members.

With the continued growth of CoDA, there was a tremendous need for development of CoDA literature, including a national newsletter and material for use in hospitals and institutions. Also needed was financial support to develop a CoDA Teen Program and to support the National Service Office.

Ken explains the overall mood of the Conference:

"There was an enormous feeling of excitement generated during those three days as CoDA's foundation was solidified in the form of a working Service Structure. Conference members returned home, charged with the responsibilities of implementing the CoDA Service Structure. By developing Group Representatives, Community Committees, State Committees and Assemblies to open the voice of CoDA to each member, we were able to establish a more effective way of communicating."

Many Conference members volunteered to serve on and support the Standing Committees of the Service Conference. It is largely through their efforts, struggles and consistency and those of succeeding Conference members, that CoDA exists today as a worldwide program. CoDA grew to approximately 4,000 meetings with a membership of approximately 100,000 within the first six years.

At the 1990 National Service Conference, Ken R. resigned as Chairperson of the Board of Trustees and as Chairperson of the Service Conference. Mary R. resigned as Trustee of the Board of Trustees. They both continued to serve as nonvoting Trustees and Advisors until fully resigning at the 1993 National Service Conference. Today they continue to be of service to CoDA as members, Founders, and as guided by a loving Higher Power.

The CoDA Service Conference has grown and expanded since its organization. The CoDA Board of Trustees has varied between seven to fifteen members. Chosen for their diverse talents, skills and abilities, Trustees demonstrate an overwhelming level of commitment to carry on the unending work of service to CoDA.

Today, the CoDA, Inc. Board is responsible for managing the day-to-day business of CoDA, responding to the service needs of the Fellowship and coordinating functions of the Conference Committees.

The CoDA Conference Committees have continued to meet the needs of the CoDA Fellowship. The current committees (as of this printing) are Hospitals & Institutions, Convention, Service Conference, Service Structure, Outreach, Literature, Finance, Co-NNections, Issues Mediation, and Translation Management. The members of each committee work diligently and lovingly, providing a tremendous amount of support, information and guidance.

The Fellowship of Co-Dependents Anonymous is and will continue to grow and expand worldwide. As it does, the needs of the Fellowship will continue to grow and expand as well. With the help of God, the volunteer service organization of CoDA and you, the individual members of CoDA, CoDA will continue to be a strong and viable worldwide resource for the support of recovery from codependency and will continue to fulfill its primary spiritual aim—to carry our message of recovery to those who still suffer from codependency, until the need to do so no longer exists.

How To Get In Touch With CoDA

For general information about CoDA,
please write or call:
Co-Dependents Anonymous, Inc.
P.O. Box 33577
Phoenix, AZ 85067-3577
USA
Phone: 602-277-7991
www.coda.org

This is CoDA Conference endorsed literature
Copyright© 2016
All Rights Reserved.
This publication may not be reproduced
or photocopied without written permission
of Co-Dependents Anonymous, Inc.

For additional copies of this book, or to order other CoDA
Conference endorsed literature, contact:
CoRe Publications
P.O. Box 1004
Denver, NC 28037-1004
USA
Phone: 704-483-3038
Fax: 704-483-3088
E-mail: coreorders@gmail.com
Online ordering: www.coda.org/index.cfm/purchase/

CoDA Materials Available from CoRe

Service Items
 Fellowship Service Manual (FSM): CoDA's Organization & Procedures

 CoDA Meeting Starter Packet

Pamphlets
 What is CoDA?

 Welcome to CoDA

 Am I Codependent?

 Attending Meetings

 Communications & Recovery

 Boundaries

Booklets & Handbooks
 Tools for Recovery Booklet

 Common Threads of Codependency Booklet

 Crosstalk Handbook

 Making Choices Booklet

 Carrying the Message–Living the 12th Step Booklet

 Peeling the Onion Booklet

 Newcomers Handbook

 Twelve Steps Handbook

 Building CoDA Community, Healthy Meetings Matter

 Sponsorship: What's in it for me?

Workbook
The Twelve Steps & Twelve Traditions Workbook

Special Items
Affirmations Booklet

Serenity Bookmarks (set of four)

Spanish Literature
Paquete Para Principiantes

Manual de Instrucciones Para Nuevos Participantes

Estableciendo Limites en la Recuperacion
¿Soy codependiente?

Books
Co-Dependents Anonymous Book

In This Moment Daily Meditation Book

CDs
The Twelve Steps

Newcomers/Sponsorship

Codependency & Shame

Ken R: I Feel Like I've Come Home

Anita F: How Empty of Me To Be So Full of You

Newcomers/Sponsorship

Pat: The Promises, Carmen N: A Pocket Full of Anger

Jim: I Didn't Need Any One, Any More, Mary: I Don't Surrender Easy

Wes: Turning Points

Hollis: Walking My Road of Happy Destiny

Karmann: Hope for a New Day, Ann D: I Thought I Would Be OK As an Adult

Larry V: Recovery is the Greatest Gift, Wally: Recovery, The Wildest Thing, Judith: CoDA is God's Program

Culle V: I Have a Family Today, Mike D: Look Inside For All Your Gifts, Sherrill S: Women's Issues

Jim: Who's Got My Soul?, Phyllis: I Met My Inner Child, Charles C: Relationships and Intimacy

Posters

Serenity Prayer

The Twelve Steps

The Twelve Traditions

CoDA Opening & Closing Prayers

Meeting Announcement Poster

Medallions

CoDA Antique Bronze Birthday/Anniversary Medallions—beginning with One Year

Chips

CoDA Colored Aluminum Acknowledgement Chips—One, Two, Three, Six, and Nine Months and Welcome Home

NOTES

NOTES